THE INTERNET

LIONS AND TIGERS AND BEARS

STRIKES BACK

GEORGE TAKEI

Lions and Tigers and Bears (The Internet Strikes Back) by George Takei

Copyright © 2013-2014 by Oh Myyy! Limited Liability Company

All rights reserved.

Printed in the United States of America

Except as permitted under the U.S. Copyright Act of 1976, no part of this publication may be reproduced, distributed, or transmitted in any form or by any means, or stored in a database or retrieval system, without the prior written permission of the publisher.

ISBN-13 (U.S. Edition): 978-0991370108

Oh Myyy! Limited Liability Company
1650 Broadway, Suite 609, New York, NY 10036
1-917-720-3289 | http://book.ohmyyy.gt/latb

Originally published by
Oh Myyy! Limited Liability Company, December 2013

Contents

Dedicated to

my husband Brad and
my merry band of staffers,
who have helped guide
this ship through the
treacherous waters of
yet another year
on the Internet.

<u>Lions and Tigers and Bears</u>

My early adventures on the Internet felt like freshman year at college. Everything was new and wondrous. I made so many new friends. And I put on seven pounds. All that sedentary time at the computer. (Okay, that last part was a fib. On the contrary, I was so active and traveled so much last year that I've never felt in better shape.) But still, like the prototypical freshman, I had to figure many things out myself. Like laundry. Only instead of having to learn how to wash and fold it, I spent much of my energies learning, well, how not to air it too openly. That first adventuresome year was the subject of *Oh Myyy — There Goes the Internet.* (Which is already on your bookshelf or on your kindle, right?)

Ah, but then came 2013. Writing the sequel is always trickier. In college, they understand this well. The term "sophomore" derives from two Greek words seemingly at odds with each other: *sophos* (meaning wise) and *moros* (meaning foolish or dull). In other words, "sophomores" are really just wise fools. That is very much how I felt throughout most of 2013.

First, the wise part. I had learned a great deal in 2012 about our fans — who they were, what they liked (and what they didn't), and how to keep them at least mildly entertained. You see, I make no bones about why I'm active on social media. I want people to *listen* to me when I talk about the subjects that matter to me, such as the Japanese American internment and marriage equality. But I know that I can't talk about those things all the time. Even my staunchest supporters would start to tune me out. "There goes Uncle George again, always spouting off about equality."

Instead I talked about matters the *fans* wanted to hear about, like Spock, Siri, and Grumpy Cat — all of which get a turn in this book. I understood that people came for the humor and stuck around for more of it, and that because of that — and *only* because of that — I had their attention, at least briefly. Once I had it, I discovered that I could speak on occasion about being a gay man married to my husband, and why we shouldn't put people in concentration camps. And people actually listened.

But keeping fans entertained and coming back for more in an increasingly crowded social media field is no simple matter. To stay relevant, you have to keep putting out great content. And "great content" is always relative; that is, you've got to stay ahead of the curve. The challenge remains this: The rest of the world isn't going to sit by and let you retain the bully pulpit easily.

Facebook itself has an interest in having great content so that its users keep coming back. After all, if the content isn't compelling, people will find somewhere else to spend their time. Ironically, Facebook has to rely upon its users to generate that content, and most user-generated content simply isn't very compelling. Just look at Vines, where everyone in the world can be a producer of the six-second video.

In order to stay in the game, I would have to step it up. Content that is engaging on Facebook gets rewarded by being shared on people's newsfeeds. Content that grabs your attention on Twitter gets retweeted. And content that "sucks" disappears into obscurity. It's like a 24/7 popularity contest.

Facebook is similar in many respects to a school yearbook, with the folks at Facebook headquarters our very own geeky yearbook committee. This is unsurprising, given that this is precisely how "Facebook" started at Harvard. And like a yearbook, every person, from the Prom King and Queen to the nerd reading *Popular Science* alone on the bleachers, is guaranteed at least one little spot in the book — his or her own inevitably awkward and lifetime cringe-worthy photo. But some people get to be all over the yearbook. In fact, it is a rule of thumb that the more popular you are, i.e., the more people who talk about you, the more times your mug shows up. So I knew that I had to keep people talking about my posts and my page, even as the number of competing pages and personalities rose exponentially.

I also learned that social media is constantly evolving, and if you don't evolve with it, you quickly become irrelevant. Remember Friendster and MySpace? They met social media death as quickly as they had risen. (Admittedly, some vestiges remain. We still say "He friended me on Facebook" — and I credit Friendster with that verbiage.)

By 2013, the space my social media once occupied had become significantly more crowded. There were many times more Facebook pages, Twitter accounts and websites focusing on humor or science or politics than there had been in 2012. These pages and sites often did a better job than I (or my staff) did in finding funny, interesting or epic things to share. Would we go the way of Netscape, a fast-rising star swallowed up in the ensuing fray? Would we become like AOL, a once hot commodity that is quaintly still used by an aging base? Not on my watch, I said.

So I asked my staffers, who have themselves increased in number over the past year, what other Facebook pages were doing, and how we might learn from them. The answer was deceptively simple: "The best pages do what you do, George. They engage with their fans. And they're staying on brand." In this sense, I felt we had done a good job, especially on Facebook. In fact, my staffers reported that many pages were copying our model of shareable memes. We had created a strong community of like-minded netizens who enjoyed my posts as well as each others' often spirited and witty commentary.

And we grew. And continued to grow. To keep up with where the fans were, we expanded to new frontiers like Tumblr, Pinterest and Google Plus. We worked with other sites like Buzzfeed and the Huffington Post to create original content. I even tried my hand at a few funny Amazon product reviews. We also understood that social media was where people were spending increasingly larger amounts of their time. Young people today, for example, often watch live television (if they watch it live at all) with both the TV *and* their laptops or tablet devices on. This way they can post in real time about what they are seeing, and watch what others are saying as well. I've done this myself a few times. It's almost more entertaining to watch your newsfeed and Twitter feed during the Oscars than the actual show.

But television isn't the only tradition being overhauled. I understand they're even inventing driverless cars over at Google, no doubt so that people can keep their eyes more glued than ever to their smartphones, or peering at virtual screens on their Google Glass wear, instead of on the road.

Speaking of which, another thing I learned was that you had to keep up with technology. My interest in this was high enough that I launched my own video channel on YouTube in connection with AARP called "Takei's Take" — on which I get to expound on the latest in gadgetry, technology and the Internet, in a way that was accessible to older viewers. It is a constant learning experience, and I am the wiser for it.

But now for the *moros* or "foolish" part. For all the time I spent on social media, by the end of 2012 it was clear that I didn't truly understand many of the risks involved, particularly how the Internet could really drive a person crazy. Sure, I'd faced trolls before, people who post outrageous comments in a bid to get attention. I knew not to feed those lest they grow in strength and audacity. But what I didn't expect was how quickly even my own fans could turn on me.

A potent example, which I discuss in depth later in this book, was when a story "broke" from one blogger, claiming that I don't write the memes that appear on my wall, and that I, in fact, pay someone else to write jokes for me. This was not only untrue, it got it completely backward. In fact, I hardly create any of my own jokes or memes. I don't even claim they're mine. I simply share what others have shared. In fact, that's been one of the Internet's biggest criticism of me: I don't post enough original material.

This I freely admit. It's the *Internet*. Everyone is sharing everything out there, and almost no one can stop it or collect on it. A 4-year old can download and then re-upload an image. If so, why not a 76-year old former *Star Trek* actor? It really doesn't take much. The trick is finding the "funny, epic or interesting" stuff worth sharing.

And yet in 2013, I learned the hard way that all this sharing, all this instantaneous news without any thought to original source, can come back to bite you. Apparently it only takes one irresponsible "news" source to publish a misleading statement under a misleading headline, such as "George Takei Uses a Ghostwriter," and even some of your most loyal fans will abandon you in droves without checking the facts or asking for your side of things.

I also did not fully understand that, the larger my fan base grew, the more it attracted certain types of fans who, apparently, viewed their "right" (to be entertained at all times, to not be offended, or to be free from any updates, photos or links that didn't fulfill *their* specific needs) as superior to *my* right to put what I want on my own page. Mind you, these weren't trolls. These were fans who had developed, for better or worse, a vested interest in the direction of my page or Twitter feed. They felt *entitled*. And they made their opinions clear. I found myself having to explain, defend, apologize and — in more cases than I care to recount — even delete posts or tweets, not necessarily to placate these fans, but because I didn't want the distraction of controversy overshadowing my mission. It just wasn't worth it.

Then there are the crazies — fans who post on my wall about their dreams in which I inevitably played some disturbing role, fans who accuse me — IN ALL CAPITAL LETTERS — of deleting their posts as if I'd violated a sacred trust, and strangers whose hatred of what I stood for, and whose desire to make that hatred clear, is more than a little scary.

Ah, the Internet is dark and full of terrors. Lions and tigers and bears, oh myyy.

And so I write this account as a survivor of my wise and foolish second year. Like the Internet itself, in this book I cover an eclectic (some might even say random) assortment of subjects, based on observations and thoughts I've collected over the past year. There are plenty of moments of utter silliness, right alongside examples that reflect the profound and astonishing complexity of our increasingly social, and increasingly connected, world.

But fear not, friends. I now walk the path with a few more companions alongside — more than five million on Facebook in fact — to help fend off those dangerous beasts in the Haunted Forest, granting to me more brains, heart and courage to the task of finding our way back home — which reminds me to leave you with this gem:

The Internet Strikes Back

I'm going to get some of my "bitching" out of the way right off the bat. As my fan base has grown, my page has attracted attention — some of it *not* so welcome. This unwanted spotlight has included pundits, bloggers, overly-opinionated fans, irresponsible journalists, spammers, pornographers, and even more than a few outright hate-mongers.

On the somewhat tamer side of things, my activities have spurred many a wonky "industry" discussion about the intellectual value (or lack thereof) that a "social medialite" such as myself brings to the virtual table. One pundit memorably referred to my Facebook posts as simply more "noise" on the Net. He was apparently upset that *his* far more considered and thoughtful content was being pushed out of fan newsfeeds by the banal material I posted, which, in his mind, comprised primarily nerdy scifi memes and LOL images of cats. (This particular pundit's own wife is an avowed fan of my page and shares my posts frequently, and apparently she would much rather be entertained by me than bored by him. Perhaps here lies the real reason behind his ire.)

To me, this kind of criticism evinces a decided lack of understanding about the way fan engagement works. To be sure, one can pen a scholarly, well-researched and, as some graduate students might even declare, compelling white paper on the "2009-2014 Outlook for Wooden Toilet Seats in Greater China" but no one outside of the author's immediate circle is likely to give it so much as a glance. By the way, look this up on Amazon — it is actually available for purchase, and I have reviewed it as follows:

FOR YEARS I HAVE SEARCHED FOR THE PERFECT AUDIO BOOK PROJECT. "SHOGUN," SOME FRIENDS SUGGESTED. "WAR AND PEACE," I'VE CONSIDERED. OR PERHAPS "GREEN EGGS AND HAM."

BUT IT WASN'T UNTIL I STUMBLED, QUITE BY CHANCE, ACROSS "THE 2009-2014 OUTLOOK FOR WOOD TOILET SEATS IN GREATER CHINA" THAT I KNEW. I KNEW.

SURE, THE TITLE AND THE FIRST FEW HUNDRED PAGES MAY SEEM OFF-PUTTING. "WHAT THE F*@K IS THIS?" BRAD DEMANDED, JUST 20 PAGES IN. "IT'S LIKE SOME KIND OF TERRIBLE GRAD SCHOOL THESIS."

BUT RIGHT AROUND PAGE 375, THE OFWTSIGC (2009-14) BECOMES A WHITE-KNUCKLED, ROLLER COASTER OF EMOTIONS

— THE SORT WE EXPECT FROM WORLD CLASS THRILLERS. INDEED, JUST WHEN YOU THINK THE AUTHOR HAS EXHAUSTED HIS DEAR READERS, AFTER WHAT SEEMS AN UNIMAGINABLY METHODICAL SURVEY OF MAINLAND CHINA'S WOOD TOILET SEAT PROJECTIONS, HE REMINDS US, EVER SO ARTFULLY, ABOUT GREATER CHINA.

TAIWAN. MACAO. HONG FRIGGING KONG.

NOW, ADMITTEDLY, THE NEAR $500 PRICE MAY BE A BIT DAUNTING, BUT ON A PER WORD BASIS, IT'S QUITE A BARGAIN. AND IMAGINE ITS USES! SENATE FILIBUSTERS WILL NEVER BE THE SAME. OFWTSIGC (2009-14) IT ALSO MAKES A TERRIFIC FATHER'S DAY GIFT FOR THAT DAD WHO "THINKS" HE HAS EVERYTHING. THIS WILL SHOW HIM, HUH.

As I said in my first book, *Oh Myyy — There Goes the Internet*, if you have something you want to say on the Net, first gather yourself an audience willing to listen. As I readily admit, my own "master plan" deploys the use of funny memes as a lure to attract and keep fans, so that every now and then I can step back up on my soapbox to speak about more serious matters. I would rather have some portion of five million fans bear with my occasional posts about the injustices of the Japanese-American internment in World War II than have a mere five hundred avid followers hanging on my every word.

Then there are the bloggers and outspoken fans who've taken to criticizing the manner in which I run my own page, tsk-tsking me for breaching some mysterious Internet protocol (of which I am apparently blithely unaware, and on which they are always happy to provide tutelage). For example, many have blasted me for my use of so-called "blind" links, where no preview of the subject article or video appears. On occasion, however, blind links can serve a useful purpose, as I discuss in greater depth later in the chapter entitled "Link Wars." I find such criticism presumptuous. These people usually threaten to "unlike" my page unless I change my ways, when they had absolutely no obligation to "like" my page, let alone click on such links, in the first place. Such threats are as empty as they are humorous; the irony is that I'd rather wave those folks a friendly good-bye anyway.

Another common criticism is that I use "shortened" URLs rather than ones bearing the actual website names. Again, there are many reasons for this, which I cover later in "Link Wars," not the least of which is that I need to keep text to a minimum for the sake of my Twitter account, which is closely linked to my Facebook. I am rather fond of my own URL, http://ohmyyy.gt, which my staffers say permits them to keep track of how many clicks are actually happening in real time — and thus what fans are responding to and what they are dismissing as uninteresting. (Facebook attempts to do this with its "Page Insights," but the interface and the data are not quite as user-friendly or accurate.)

As I mentioned in the introduction, some of the

most irksome comments come from those who believe that they have a right to dictate the content I choose to place on my own page. Their common complaint — and I see this almost every day — goes something like this: "Takei, I use to like u, but all u talk now is gay shit. Bye." Or, "More funnies, less blah blah please." Others complain bitterly if I so much as suggest they buy a fundraiser t-shirt or support a charity, or if I promote my own musical or book (like this one), even on my own page. "I came here for the laughs, not to be guilted," "This page used to be pure entertainment" and "Yes, we get it, George. You have a book. Now shut up about it."

Even fans who admittedly like my page and my posts sometimes take issue when I elect to do any kind of promotion. In one instance, I was offering fans a free download of a wonderful song from *Allegiance*, sung by my co-star, the incomparable Lea Salonga, which they otherwise would have had to pay for. Here is my post:

If you're having trouble reading the text in the

image, here is the text of my status update and the fan comment:

*A MOST BEAUTIFUL SONG, SUNG BY A MOST BEAUTIFUL ANGEL. AND IT'S A **FREE** DOWNLOAD TODAY, FRIENDS. YOU'LL SEE WHY I'M TERRIBLY, TERRIBLY EXCITED FOR THIS. [LINK]*

[COMMENT] I LOVE MOST OF YOUR POSTS BUT I'M SO OVER EVERY ONE OF THEM ENDING IN A LINK TO YOUR BOOK OR YOUR PLAY. CAN'T IT EVER JUST BE ABOUT SOMETHING FUN OR FUNNY WITHOUT YOU PLUGGIN YOURSELF?

Of course, it was pure exaggeration on this fan's part to suggest that "every" one of my posts ends in a link to my book or my play. Indeed, that accounts for a mere fraction of my posts. She was "so over" it, apparently, because it couldn't "ever just be about something fun or funny" any more. Apparently, she'd missed the four *other* posts that day that were purely for fun. (By the way, I did not miss the fact that "Ryan Reynolds" liked my link. Oh myyy.)

I am grateful, however, for fans who come to my defense in moments like these, reminding these hangers-on that I am not exclusively set up for their own entertainment. Here were some fan responses to that reader's particularly whiny post:

Roy C. Johnson Uncle George Takei - I loved the opportunity to download this song from your play, Allegiance!
Like · 👍 30 · December 4 at 3:47pm

Tiffani Baker Wow! Is she serious? Keep on pluggin Mr. Takei!
Like · 👍 41 · December 4 at 3:48pm

Ryan Murphy I hate to say this, but "Oh my."
Like · 👍 21 · December 4 at 3:50pm · Edited

Deborah DiClementi BTW...it's supporting a truly WONDERFUL singer who, because she happens to be Asian, is limited in what is written for her and BTFW the fact that Allegiance even exists is a treasure so that we get to hear this true angelic voice. I could BE more pissed but I don't see how. ARGH
Like · 👍 25 · December 4 at 3:50pm

And again, if your eyes, like mine, are growing too weak to decipher the above, here is the text of the comments for your convenience:

> UNCLE GEORGE TAKEI - *I* LOVED THE OPPORTUNITY TO DOWN-LOAD THIS SONG FROM YOUR PLAY, ALLEGIANCE!

> WOW! IS SHE SERIOUS? KEEP ON PLUGGING MR. TAKEI!

> *I* HATE TO SAY THIS, BUT "OH MY."

> BTW.... IT'S SUPPORTING A TRULY **WONDERFUL** SINGER WHO, BECAUSE SHE HAPPENS TO BE ASIAN, IS LIMITED IN WHAT IS WRITTEN FOR HERE AND **BTFW** THE FACT THAT ALLEGIANCE EVEN EXISTS IS A TREASURE SO THAT WE GET TO HEAR THIS TRUE ANGELIC VOICE. *I* COULD **BE** MORE PISSED BUT *I* DON'T SEE HOW. **ARGH**

For some time I would try to explain, with as much patience as I could muster, that yes, I *do* indeed have an agenda: to discuss issues of equality and justice, and to promote my show *Allegiance* (indeed, that was the very reason I got started in social media). If they can't give a bit of their time to listen to my spiel, then they are free to ignore me. I also find myself having to remind fans that, as to matters like my book, I am self-published and therefore some amount of sales pitch is necessary, that I nevertheless attempt to make each promotion as entertaining as I can, and that they are under absolutely no obligation to buy anything, let alone click on an ad. If it's easy enough to fast-forward through commercials on your DVR, it is surely just as easy to scroll past a post that you don't want to click. And if I happen to have piqued fan curiosity with my description of a link, I suppose it's up to them whether they want to click it or not.

Lately, I've concluded that it is precisely *because* I have made an effort to render even my promotional posts amusing that I receive this level of fan push-back. If someone spends even two seconds of their online time clicking on what amounts to a promotion for my book, this means, in their own mind, that they were had, because all they ever expect and want from me is more free funnies. The irony, of course, is that the very next thing they do is waste minutes of their bitter and embattled lives crafting a long and wrenching complaint about their experience of having been bamboozled into clicking on an advertisement. No matter that Facebook itself is now replete with sponsored ads that no one signs up to see, and which take up space on our newsfeeds unbidden. These are the same fans who believe that everything in life should come to them free of charge and perfectly explained and laid out for them to enjoy. In fact, my occasional promotion of my book is precisely what *does* permit them to enjoy my funnies for free.

The online media has plagued me with its own set of exasperating practices. Despite being self-appointed "Internet journalists," who presumably spend much if not all of their professional lives scouring the web, some members of the online press demonstrate distressingly unprofessional and unsavvy journalistic methodologies, which, in my view, even border on unethical. The most startling example of this I detail later in this book in "Ghostwriters on the Storm," where a misinterpreted statement (by someone I've never even spoken to or met) was reposted by a single blogger, then churned into a full-blown false story by the online media, which was repeated often enough by others that it became in their minds the truth.

Another example of irresponsible net journalism showed a decided lack of understanding of the way Facebook works and the way I manage my posts, which happily is increasingly under the careful guidance of my net-savvy staffers. During the New York City 2013 mayoral campaign, I endorsed Supervisor Christine Quinn for mayor, who would have been the first lesbian mayor of a major (indeed, *the* major) U.S. city. I wasn't expecting that my endorsement of her would be met with quite such a hue and cry by supporters of her primary opponent, Bill de Blasio (who later defeated his Republican opponent and is now mayor). "Stay out of our politics, George!" "Don't back her just because she's a lesbian, dude" and "DISLIKE, UNFRIEND" were common wall comments. Politics is never an easy subject, and it's even more difficult online. As to staying out of NYC politics, why should I? I noted patiently to fans that I own an apartment in New York, pay local and state taxes there, and consider myself to be actively involved in many New York matters, not the least of which is my upcoming Broadway-bound musical *Allegiance*, and thus have as much right as anyone to have an opinion on New York politics.

The most curious upshot of my endorsement, however, was an article that gleefully observed that my endorsement post had only garnered "a few thousand likes" on Facebook, rather than the typical tens of thousands my other posts generally receive, and then breathlessly concluded that this proved "even George Takei can't save Christine Quinn." This was Internet journalism at its poorest. If the reporter (who, by the way, was from a major news media outlet) had bothered to contact me, or any member of my staff for that matter, he would have learned that I intentionally had limited my endorsement geographically to the state of New York, so the base of fans who would even be seeing the post was just a fraction of my total. I learned last year that geographic targeting of posts was possible, and thus, at appropriate times, my staff has helped me limit individual posts to their intended audiences. After all, why place a local political endorsement for a NYC mayoral race onto the already busy newsfeeds of fans in Missouri or Luxembourg?

Add to that the fact that, among even those fans located within Greater New York, there would be many who would not be voting in the primary (for example, independent, Libertarian, Green or Republican voters) and therefore simply would not be that interested in the Democratic candidate for mayor and no reason to voice their opinion on my endorsement. I was actually quite pleased with the number of "likes" my limited endorsement post received. But that didn't stop the media from running with the story that a perceived tepid response to my endorsement spelled the doom of the endorsed candidate.

Another constant battle I wage these days is against spammers. With nearly every post I make, someone in the world is ready to comment not with words germane to the post or to the dialogue among fans, but with promotions of their own businesses or causes, or worse still, with malware or a link designed to ensnare unwitting fans. The peskiest of these spammers offers fans the opportunity to "Change their Facebook Page Color" to one of their own choosing. My understanding is that this is just a "phishing scam" to gather user data, but the dangerously clever part lies in the fact that it is programmed to appear at or near the top of every comment stream and thus is far more likely to trick the unwary. By way

27

of background, sometime in 2013, Facebook began to reward "popular" comments (that is, comments with many likes or replies) by placing them at or near the top of the comment stream. The scam in question leveraged that functionality by automatically giving itself numerous likes, ensuring its placement as a top comment. The only way to rid the stream of this spam was to monitor each and every post, delete the offending spam and ban the user. The problem was, however, that even after being banned under one account, the spammers would simply create a new account and begin the process all over again.

But even this was not as annoying as the pornographers. These woeful miscreants began taking to my wall to post messages that often read something like this:

< ---------- *WATCH FREE SEX VIDEO*

with the arrow pointing straight at a profile pic that, shall we say, plainly violated Facebook community standards. Again, deleting each post off the wall (and there were usually ten or so per day) and even banning the offending poster did nothing to stop the pornographic appropriation of my wall, because the porn purveyors simply created a new account and resumed their "porn bombs." I felt as if we were guiding a ship that increasingly was overburdened with clingy barnacles that we had to scrub off each day by hand. The situation eventually became so intolerable that we elected to hide the fan wall post box from the page, so that they are now accessible only if you elect the "Other Posts" view.

The necessity of this step was made even more abundantly clear by the rise in outright hate speech on my wall, which often carried with it the ugly threat of stalker psychosis and violence that only the use of ALL CAPS N ODD ABBREVS CAN DO 2 U. My own thoughts turned to the young people who look to my posts and my page as a place of acceptance and support, and how if we weren't vigilant about deleting and banning such hate, they might yet again have to endure it, even on a page dedicated to the opposite result. I might be 76 years old and relatively impervious to this kind of immaturely-expressed hate and vitriol, but I am well aware of the effect such words might have on a young person still coming to terms with his or her sexuality. With the rise of online bullying and associated teen suicide, I don't want my page to play any part in that.

And so, the sub-title of this book is "The Internet Strikes Back" for a reason. Like the Force, there is both a light and a dark side to this all-encompassing phenomenon. And there is always the danger that the dark side, with all of its allure, pain and terror will win. But not on my watch, friends. Not on my watch.

Admiral Snackbar

To the chagrin of certain of my co-stars, it's often the supporting characters who steal the show. Among scifi nerds, one of the most beloved is Admiral Gial Ackbar, who famously led the rebel forces on a mission to destroy the Death Star II in *Star Wars: Return of the Jedi*. Admiral Ackbar is recognizable throughout scifidom for his singular exclamation, "IT'S A TRAP!" These words were uttered when it became clear that the Imperial Forces had been awaiting the rebel assault. Despite the odds, Admiral Ackbar did not sound the retreat, and though they suffered heavy losses, the rebels succeeded in their mission, and the rebuilt Death Star was no more.

In the movie, we learn very little about Ackbar.

Why is he an admiral? What grudge does he hold against the Empire? And why is his name spelled with an extra "c"? Indeed, despite his high recognition among *Star Wars* fans (and thus, humanity in general), very little is known about Admiral Ackbar beyond his most attributed utterance. But, again, like that little old lady in the Wendy's burger commercial — one line is enough. Indeed, the phrase, "IT'S A TRAP!" has now become uniquely associated with Admiral Ackbar. Just try saying it without thinking of him. It's impossible.

Part of the appeal has got to be his delivery. Admiral Ackbar, let's face it, resembles a squid, making the name of his race, the *Mon Calamari*, rather curious, and not only for its awkward mix of French and Italian. As a result of his physical limitations, his speech is, well, a bit muddled by excess flaps of skin, a particularly wide mouth and wobbly gullet. Your mind's ear can easily hear him bellow it now: "IT'S A TRWAPP!"

As these things so often go, the Internet decided to seize upon Admiral Ackbar and his well-known exclamation and produce several hilarious spoofs. One of my favorites is by cartoonist Scott Johnson (with the idea from Mark Turpin). They imagine that, after destroying the Death Star II, Admiral Ackbar has fallen upon hard times and taken to selling roadside food at a stand:

By the bye, this scores triple points from me: 1) fine wordplay on his name (Snackbar is just too, too good), 2) fine wordplay on his signature phrase, and 3) backstory on what happened to him after *Return of the Jedi*. If this were an MTV special on "Where Are They Now," the galaxy could shake its collective heads at how far the mighty have fallen. (For more funnies by Scott, visit his website at myextralife. com).

Another meme imagines the Admiral as a spokesman for Starbucks Coffee, which apparently has left the confines of Terran soil and expanded, as surprised no one, to the far reaches of the Galactic Empire. In fact, I've heard that on the Death Star there are over 100 Starbucks franchises, sometimes one just on the other side of a blast door from another. May the froth be with you:

This one scores points for the detail on the Rebel Alliance insignia on the logo and the cup — and makes the difference between laughing at the joke and being totally in on it. The backstory here, of course, is presumably quite different: Having successfully led the assault upon the Death Star II, Admiral Ackbar can now write his own endorsement deals! And who better than a Starship Admiral to be the new face of *Starbucks*? After all, is it really that great a leap from a mermaid to a *calamari?*

I had some fun of my own posting an Admiral Ackbar meme. I know from experience that some of my most popular updates are those that forge unexpected bonds among fans. How many fans, I wondered, would "get" this possibly obscure pop reference? (I added the caption, "You know you want to say it.")

Turns out, nearly 70,000 fans "got" it, and more importantly, another 22,000-some shared it. And this got me to pondering: What causes people to like and share these kinds of images?

Sure, they're funny. But there are lots of funnies out there on the Internet. What a funny like this does is something more. Perhaps it says, "Ah, this was a part of my childhood." Or "I took my children to see this." Liking it means you're part of a club, an instant community, if you will. We all mysteriously remember this precise moment in Episode VI of *Star Wars* where this supporting character warned, "It's a trap!" and charged ahead anyway.

But *sharing* this image means something else, too. That act not only says, "I find this funny," but also "I think you, my friends, will find this funny, and possibly 'like' it too, because we have a similar sense of humor and a common background. Moreover, if something is both funny and "cool," and someone finds it on the Internet, that "find" has some value. So when that "find" is shared, that act itself is one of generosity (or, for the more cynically-minded, a way to affirm and broadcast your coolness). Finally, sharing something someone cool has shared — someone, say, with a great number of friends on Facebook — might also lend some coolness to the sharer, dare I suggest. Cool by association has always been a ticket into the "in" crowd in high school, and in life.

To extend the pop-up community that formed around this single image, fans presented their favorite Admiral Akbar memes in the comment stream below the image. Because Facebook now rewards "top" comments (those with the most likes and/or replies) with "top" placement, the best material can literally float to the top and be enjoyed by anyone who wants to stay and play a bit longer. Here was what rose to the top in response to one of my posts:

It's actually hard not to smile at the notion of Admiral Akbar holding this and shouting "It's a tarp!" There's a good chance you probably just heard that in his voice, in fact. That the top comment to my post itself got over 2,400 likes tells me that many, many fans understand the absurdity of their random connectedness through the good *mon calamari.*

Other fans chimed in with their favorites. On the low-brow end of things, there was this, dare I say it, "nugget" which many uber-fans insisted they wanted to replicate on their own toilets:

Here again, extra points for a font and design that evoke the franchise.

Among the other submissions, I preferred this next one, in part because it mixes two of my favorite genres (Broadway and scifi), but also because it demands a bit more cultural literacy from its viewer:

Finally, recently I checked my Facebook wall, and someone had pointed out that there is an odd connection between our current president and the admiral. I imagine many might stare at these images without getting the joke, so some textual context was added.

Ah. Perhaps now we know why he spells his name that way.

<u>Earworms</u>

We've all had them: songs, or bits of songs, stuck in our heads that we can't seem to shake, except possibly by substituting *another* song, which merely replaces one problem with another. These are what we call earworms—sneaky, burrowing little bugs that cause something inside our brains to repeat a ditty over and over, as though teetering on lunacy.

Earworms are not only bothersome, they are highly contagious. All it takes is one person humming the chorus of "We Built This City" to get a whole room thinking, "on Rock and Rooooooooll!" In fact, merely reading the words "We Built This City" may have already infected your own ears, just now, with that insipid melody.

I figured, if a room can be infected by just one person, what would happen on the Internet? In theory, by way of a single viral post, hundreds of thousands of people literally could be tuned to the same musical wavelength, not just in America but all around the world. For the earworm, properly planted, is far more than an individual, personal experience. It is quintessentially communal. The songs we all knew and loved in our earlier, more carefree days could at any moment come crashing back upon us, even from just a single line of a song. By some twisted trick of nature, we recall not just the tune, ah, but the lyrics! This is possible even though we can't remember what we ate for breakfast, how to do long division, or where we put our keys just ten minutes past.

Given just the right earworm, our collective heads could bang up and down together, our imagined younger selves air-guitaring in perfect synch as if we didn't have children, mortgages or hip surgeries to occupy our thoughts and energies. Speaking of air guitars, this image made me want to grab one:

But back to my first example. "We Built This City" was the international 1980s hit by the group Starship, which is the curious and sad vestige of the more awesome and wholly legitimate Jefferson Airplane. It formed after every original band member of Jefferson Airplane had departed and filed the requisite lawsuits. The song enjoyed a strong showing on the charts, but years later many have come to consider it the worst rock song ever, in that it is both completely inane *and* completely unforgettable. *Rolling Stone* readers in fact voted it the worst song of the 1980s, and by a landslide. This pretty much heralded the doom of 1980s-style rock music, much as Disco Demolition Night on July 29, 1979 marked the end of the boogie era.

When I posted about this particular earworm, though, I really had just one question:

I've learned from my fans that they share a love/ hate relationship to the earworm. I often like to post earworms at the start of the work day, when the mind is most susceptible to suggestion, and when a particularly pesky ditty is most likely to linger—through traffic jams, conference calls, and team meetings in windowless conference rooms. Many fans delight in completing them:

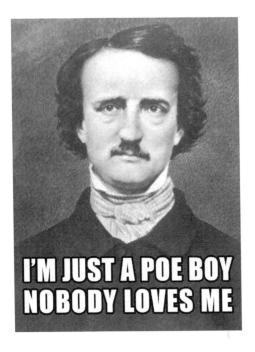

I'M JUST A POE BOY
NOBODY LOVES ME

Their eager response: "He's just a Poe boy from a Poe family!!"

Other fans are less amused by my earworms and will let me know it. "I hate you." "Great. Now that will be stuck in my head. All. Day." "Why, Uncle George. WHY????!!!!"

Fans sent in their own earworms, sometimes in the form of puzzles. Now, because songs tend to be generational, I'd often give those born after 1980 a bit more time to solve some of the older ones. Here was one example:

Like their cousins, the "terribly bad puns," ear-worms are as likely to receive groans as they are smiles. I've done a bit of thinking on this. IMHO, we groan at puns because we sense, deep in our souls, that there has been some egregious violation of the rules forbidding the base exploitation of language. Indeed, the pun is considered by many to be more distasteful than the common expletive. You might even say the pun is mightier than the s-word.

Unlike puns, however, earworms exploit music instead of language. They borrow from the same tra-dition. Speaking of musical puns, this reminds me of something borderline criminal:

The hybrid "punny" earworm began making its way onto my Facebook wall sometime in 2013, as fans tracked down some of the worst offenders and shared them. This confirmed for me that the two phenomena were closely linked. One in particular was a clear triumph—a perfect storm of pun, earworm, and the Internet's favorite food, bacon:

This devious meme had the effect of causing a trifecta in many: a low groan from the pun, a deep grumble from the stomach, and a shared madness from thousands singing, "Don't go bacon my, don't go bacon my..." for the rest of the morning.

Speaking of food-related earworms, another fan favorite was this:

There is something timeless about this particular Eurythmics song. The lyrics are haunting, even if they make no sense, so it was easy pickings for pun enthusiasts. It also is quite easy to hear Annie Lennox singing these cheese lyrics in place of the real ones. How curious the brain is. I'll bet you're doing it right now.

Related to the earworm is the mistaken lyric. These can be quite fun, and funny, and they bind us together in collective and honest mistaken error as powerfully as the songs themselves do.

Here are some of my favorites. Can you identify the original tune?

The phenomenon of misheard lyrics really ought to be fading, as the Internet gives anyone the opportunity to search for the correct version. But few bother, it seems, happy in their ignorance, crowing Pat Benetar's "Hit me with your rickshaw!" and getting down to the Beegee's "Your man's a woman. Your man's a woman to me..."

What's even odder is how so many can make the *same* mistake with the *same* lyrics. Many startled listeners likely simply assumed Jimmy Hendrix was professing his bisexuality with, "'Scuse me, while I kiss this guy." Or that Clarence Clearwater Revival was warning of serial rest stop murderers with their ominous, "Don't go out tonight, or it's bound to take your life. There's a bathroom on the right."

Darn it, now those songs are stuck in *my* head.

Ghostwriters on the Storm

I'd like to set the record straight. If there's one thing I've made perfectly clear ever since I began my new "trek" across social media, it is this: Almost none of the humor I post is actually my own. I have always been someone who enjoys *other* people's humor and shares it, often quite liberally, with just a caption or a comment on why I found it funny. I still find it incredible that anyone would assume I am sitting at my computer playing with Photoshop and creating the "funnies" that appear on my Facebook page and Twitter stream. No, I can't and won't take credit for the humor; it is 99% OPS — Other People's Stuff.

For this, I have been lambasted by critics and even a few "fans" who decry my woeful lack of originality. "All George Takei does is share stuff already out there." "Saw this already on [9GAG] [Reddit] [4chan]" (sites I never visit, by the way). "Hey, I posted that yesterday, George. Where's the credit?"

Try as I could to explain that I wasn't in the business of being an original comic, and that at most I am merely curating and picking material I find funny, the Internet had — and continues to have — a hard time grasping this. Over the past year, nearly every day I'd receive some kind of complaint that I was a plagiarist or, as the page admin of a popular science page once quipped, "a thieving bastard" (ironically for sharing memes that she had probably gotten from another site). This type of criticism was both annoying for its frequency and disheartening for completely missing the mark. For isn't Facebook a place to share all manner of things, from the funny to the thought-provoking, the personal to the political, the maddening to the inspirational? And couldn't I participate in this free-wheeling market, just as everyone else does? Ah, the price of even modest fame; I became a target simply because *more people* saw the things I shared.

So I turned to my staffers to ask if there was anything to be done.

And yes, to set another record straight, I **do** have staffers — at first some interns, and lately some paid help. Again, it seems axiomatic that someone with my speaking and acting schedule, with more than six million fans across Facebook, Twitter, Google+, Pinterest and Tumblr, would hire a bit of help to make sure things run smoothly. Without "Team Takei," which includes my very patient husband Brad, there would be no way to sift through the mountains of emails and wall posts I receive, or to edit my blog, schedule my posts while I'm busy in studio or on stage, and keep track of all the various platforms.

But back to the question of "original humor." One of my staffers suggested back in 2012 that we could ask the fans themselves to contribute their own original memes, so that we'd be the first to share them and other sites might start being accused of stealing our posts instead. I thought, why not? Let's give it a try. So we invited our base to submit not just things they'd found elsewhere, but new humor that we could share with the fans.

I encouraged this practice by noting that certain memes were "from a fan" — that is, typically, a fan had sent it to me via email or posted it on my Facebook wall. I honestly had no idea in each instance whether the humor was original or not, and could hardly keep up with the number of submissions, so there really was no way to ascribe credit, if credit was in fact due. At best, if someone complained that they should have been credited, and provided some evidence that they'd actually created something I had posted, my staffers could go back and edit the caption to include a name or a link.

(By the way, this is a small beef I have with Facebook. Have you ever wondered why can page admins edit the caption of a photo or a comment to a status, but not the actual status itself? Individuals have this ability with their status updates, but Pages like mine do not. There is nothing worse than hitting "Post" and then seeing a glaring typo. Try doing that where millions of people stand ready to correct your spelling.)

As time went on, it was apparent that there were a handful of prolific meme-generators. One of these was Rick Polito, a humorist who apparently specialized in satirizing television shows and movies. At the recommendation of my staff, I'd shared a number of his funny write-ups, sent fans to his Facebook page, and even gave him a plug in my last book.

Now, I'm not one to take advantage of people's work without compensation. Although I'd never met Mr. Polito, when one of my staffers told me that Mr. Polito was interested in being a regular contributor of memes, but that he was a struggling single dad who'd been out of work for some time, I agreed with my staffer's suggestion that we could pay him something modest — perhaps ten dollars — for each original funny image he created that we actually used. In my mind, this was a win/win situation: Perhaps we'd get some new humor to share instead of just resharing existing memes, and Mr. Polito would get some kind of compensation for his efforts.

Regrettably, this arrangement with Mr. Polito didn't really work out. He submitted a few memes to my team, which rejected most of them as too off-color. I believe we ended up using just a few of images, and our staffer paid Mr. Polito something like forty dollars before breaking the news that it really wasn't working out.

That was the last I'd heard, until *Wired* magazine published an outrageous article claiming that Rick Polito was George Takei's "ghostwriter."

Excuse me?

It appears Mr. Polito, whom I understand was attempting to gain some publicity for a book he'd recently authored, had spoken to a single blogger and "revealed" in that conversation that he'd been paid $10 per "joke" by George Takei. Now, technically, this could be construed as true — we did pay him for submitting some memes we actually used. But what followed from this was Internet "journalism" at its worst. From being paid for a few submissions of funny images to someone on my staff, Mr. Polito suddenly went to being a "ghostwriter" for my entire page.

Mind you, I'd never met Mr. Polito, or even spoken to him. But, as these things go on the Internet, once one news organization says "ghostwriter," everyone else piles on without bothering to check their facts.

I felt very annoyed by the whole affair, and wrote a quick email to *Wired*:

> **WHAT IS THIS HOO-HA ABOUT MY FACEBOOK POSTS? I HAVE BRAD, MY HUSBAND, TO HELP ME, AND INTERNS TO ASSIST. WHAT IS IMPORTANT IS THE RELIABILITY OF MY POSTS BEING THERE TO GREET MY FANS WITH A SMILE OR A GIGGLE EVERY MORNING. THAT'S HOW WE KEEP ON GROWING.**

By this I wanted to emphasize, as I did in my first book, that of *course* I have help on my page, especially with sifting through of fan mail and postings which happen throughout the day. At the same time, I asked my staffer to get in touch with Mr. Polito and seek clarification. Surely he didn't mean to claim he wrote for my Facebook page, or that he was in any way a "ghostwriter." That was an outrageous distortion. As we all knew, the only thing he'd done was to create memes like so many other fans do; our mistake was that we offered to pay him something small for his efforts, since he claimed to rely on his comedy for his living and claimed to be out of work. (Ironically, had we *not* paid him for his images, this would never have happened. And here we were, thinking we were being kind.)

Meanwhile, the Internet swirled with the "scandal" that *Wired* had ignited: "Polito, George Takei's ghostwriter!" Now as far as I understand, a "ghostwriter" sits in the place of the actual person, penning material on his behalf on a regular basis. The idea that Mr. Polito was such a person, given that I'd never even met the fellow, struck me as particularly irresponsible for anyone to claim or report.

But knowing how online rumors work, and how any attempt to correct the record usually only fuels the feeding frenzy, I decided to try to remain above the fray. My true fans knew and understood that my Facebook page is my own, and that I have a team of helpers to assist me in keeping it going. They also knew that I was already squarely in the business of sharing *other* people's memes, and that therefore there was never any "writing" to be had in the first instance, unless you count my blog which is certainly nothing Mr. Polito ever came near. If *Wired* were to be believed, Mr. Polito was busy at his home office somewhere pretending to be me and holding himself out to millions of fans. How absurd.

I thought the matter would die down after Mr. Polito wrote to my staffer and apologized for inadvertently causing a maelstrom, through a misunderstood and off-hand remark to a single blogger. That apology was conveyed to me, and I thought the matter done and over. But no, apparently seeking again to bring attention to his book, the following week Mr. Polito spoke again to the blogger, saying this:

> *"I WROTE AN APOLOGY TO GEORGE AND BRAD, AND THEIR GUY SAID HE'D PASS IT ON. I JUST SAID THAT I'D BEEN LOOKING FOR ANY MENTION OF MY BOOK I COULD GET, AND THAT I HADN'T MEANT TO EXPOSE ANYTHING.*
>
> *I DON'T UPDATE HIS PAGE. I'VE HAD NO DIRECT CONTACT WITH GEORGE. I'VE SENT HIM SOME MEMES, AS HAVE OTHER COMEDIAN TYPES, AND I WAS HAPPY FOR THE EXPOSURE."*

Proving again that the Internet can create a mountain out of any molehill, the web site mashable.com turned this apology into a *second* story with this unfortunate headline: "George Takei's Facebook Ghostwriter Apologizes."

Good grief. Suddenly, I was again paired with Mr. Polito as my "ghostwriter," who now was "apologizing" for "revealing" his work with me? If anyone had bothered to read what Mr. Polito actually said, they would have concluded that he could not by any stretch be called a ghostwriter simply for sending in some memes.

No matter. That misleading *mashable* headline was picked up by all manner of other media, from the *Hollywood Reporter* to local TV news affiliates, not one of which ever bothered to try and contact me to get my side of things. It was truly Orwellian: By publishing and republishing the same mistake, it had become true in the eyes of the world.

I explained on my Facebook page, in comment threads, and in response to fan posts that the story was complete hogwash, that I've never met or even spoken with Mr. Polito, and that people shouldn't believe everything they read on the Internet. But I've come to understand that it's nearly impossible to stop an Internet rumor, especially if it's backed up by "reputable" media. And on a slow news day, an "apology" from an alleged "ghostwriter" on a popular Facebook page unfortunately passes for a top headline.

In the end, I suppose it doesn't really matter what people believe about my page or who helps make sure it's functional. As busy as I've gotten, I barely have the time to go through what my staffers and Brad put together for me daily to review and comment on, let alone deal with this kind of garbage "journalism." As I told *Wired* magazine, all that really matters is that the funnies on my page continue to delight and entertain fans. Inevitably, there will be others who are credited for things that are mine, or media outlets that sensationalize or distort facts beyond recognition. That's just the price of being a public figure these days, especially on social media.

Spock You Like A Hurricane

Spock is, without doubt, one of the most memorable and iconic figures in science fiction—or any fiction for that matter. His cool logic and dispassionate mien represent some kind of higher ideal for humans, reminding us that we can and must leave behind our primitive "lizard" brains in order to experience what more evolved species are destined to enjoy—the pleasures of the mind.

Lately, the old Vulcan from the original *Star Trek* started making a comeback, in part because of the franchise reboot. But the comeback was not in the way you would expect. Spock started to become a popular meme precisely because he was so, well, "un-Spock-like" at times.

63

Here's what I mean by that. Fans of Mr. Logical found some classic moments from the original series (or as fans refer to it, *Star Trek: TOS*) and began to have some fun with them. These moments weren't your typical Spock scenes—e.g., calmly reminding Kirk not to be rash or emotional, coolly and quickly calculating the odds of surviving something cataclysmic, or failing to see the humor in something obviously hilarious. Rather, these were moments where Spock was decidedly out-of-character, so much so that we could imagine he was, deep down, more like us.

Might, for example, Spock weep at the end of chick flicks? Could he be uncontrollably ticklish? Might he have insatiable cravings for sinful foods like chocolate or bacon? And might he even be prone to sudden outbursts of, say, rock music and head banging, when a song comes on the radio?

ROOOOXAAANNNEEEE...!!

In short, might it be that in his most private moments, Spock sets aside Vulcan heritage and upbringing and taps into his very human half?

The above image reminds me that the pairing of Spock with modern day lyrics and bands is something of a "thing" on the Internet these days. These resonate in a particular way because they cross a rather deep generational divide—a beloved figure from the 1960s/70s and the hippest (and in many cases loudest) music of today. I found that the more outrageous the pairing, the more popular the meme became.

In this example, it's just plain hard to view the image without a certain earworm popping into your head:

The very metal band Scorpions from Germany probably had little idea that they would share their lyrics with Spock. The pun of course doesn't hurt.

Then there's this one, which amazingly crossed *two* music generations, venturing into Elecrtro-House.

LMFAO indeed. (If you don't know that group, or what those letters mean, I recommend you look it up. Do not under any circumstances ask your teenager.)

My favorite Spock humor took "urban" lyrics and rewrote them with a Spockian twist. I enjoyed posting these on my page, challenging my fans to see how many of them would "get" them. And okay, I admit it, I occasionally had to seek the assistance of younger staff members to decode these memes for me. Here are two that made the rounds in this quadrant of the galaxy:

 My dairy-based frozen confection creates a focal point to which young males of the species are drawn. You are correct: it is far superior to yours. I could attempt to educate you on the finer points of this subject, but it would require monetary recompense on your part.

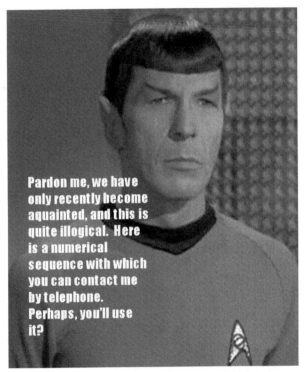

These memes were popular not only for their juxtaposition of the presumably placid Spock with the decidedly raunchy or bubble-gum pop lyrics, but also because they "gameified" the moment. Puzzles like this, which ask fans to *think,* have their own rewards when solved. They are also most likely to be shared, as fans subconsciously wonder whether their own friends and families are as nerdy, bright and culturally attuned as they are. The "share" that results from these types of gameified posts in fact helps coalesce an otherwise ragtag, random base into one that identifies as cross-generational, savvy and clever.

Taking up the theme of Spock and the beats and tunes of our modern day life, an image of Spock mixing tracks as an actual D.J. wasn't far behind. He actually shares this honor with Professor Snape of Harry Potter fame, and indubitably for the same reason: When you think of that hostile head of Slytherin House, with his signature deadpan delivery, this image of Snape at the turntablemight be the furthest thing from your mind:

Now tell me you didn't just read that in his chilling manner.

The Spock version of this, on the other hand, had the advantage of providing one of the worst puns I've ever seen.

SPACE
the vinyl frontier

Let me go on "record" as saying, this puts quite a new spin on things.

Then there is our fascination with what I have dubbed "The Sensual Spock." If you've ever walked in on parents "doing it," you will not soon shake that image from your mind. If this never happened to you, count yourself lucky. In a similar vein, we are at once repulsed and transfixed by the idea of "Spock Sex." Few have ever seen Spock in anything less than a full Starfleet uniform, so viewing his startlingly hirsute, naked torso, in what can best be described as the beginnings of a Nazi bondage porno, can be rather disquieting, to say the least:

We also never like to think of Vulcans as descended from primates as we "primat-ive" humans are, so this image is all the more incongruous. Spock has always been so successful at burying and shrouding his half-human heritage, with all that unseemly emotion, that we often forget that he shares our simian DNA, at least in part. Still, I've found this image can only be erased from our minds by adding a touch of Vulcan humor to the mix, as one of my favorite Star Trek memes did quite successfully:

71

Now isn't that better?

Another popular meme is of Spock in the company of a small black cat. If memory serves me, this image is from a scene in an episode called "Catspaw" from the second season of *Star Trek: The Original Series.* It stands to reason that Vulcans might prefer cats over more emotionally-available and eager-to-please dogs; Spock would never approve of the unbridled and unconditional love and exuberance so typical of canines. Cats, on the other hand, are similar to Vulcans—dispassionate, contemplative and pointy-eared.

His apparent affection for cats is shared with his *Star Trek: The Next Generation* counterpart, the android Data, whose pet cat bore the awkward name of Spot.

Cats

The preferred pets of logical beings.

In the reboot of the *Star Trek* movies, Spock has an improbably and steamy romantic relationship with Lieutenant Uhura. As shocking as it maybe to witness a Vulcan acting like a teenager with all the attendant raging hormones, he wouldn't be the first *Star Trek* character to "get down" with Uhura. Kirk and Uhura shared the first black/white kiss ever aired on TV (another milestone for the series). Only I seemed immune to her raw sexiness (for reasons no one knew at the time), as the winning entry from my on-line "Caption This!" contest summed up brilliantly:

As a final note, I'd be remiss if I didn't point out that the "new" Spock in the *Star Trek* movies, Zachary Quinto, is an openly gay actor, something that would have been unthinkable back when *Star Trek: The Original Series* aired. Perhaps the greatest thing about this fact is that, while it was met with enthusiastic "squees" from LGBT fans, the news largely received a collective shrug from straight ones. How far we have come.

After all, as Spock might say, judging someone's acting based on his sexual orientation is quite illogical.

Grumpy Cat

Those who follow my Facebook page know that, like the rest of the Internet, a good percentage of my posts are about cats. Brad and I actually feed and care for three feral cats — Fluffy, Ginger and Evil Eyes — who have made our yard in Los Angeles their home. In my first book, I devoted a whole chapter to humanity's furred, feline friends and their conquest of the Internet. But I'd like to take a moment to give credit to the one puss that, in a very short time, has become not only the most popular *felis catus* in the world, but also one of its most recognizable personalities: Grumpy Cat.

If you haven't seen Grumpy Cat, you haven't been paying attention. Her unique mug appears daily

75

in tens of thousands of newsfeeds, blogs, and posts. Grumpy Cat's mien is so distinctive, and so compelling, that she has become a cultural icon. And it took her less than a year.

From this emerged countless memes. Fans took her apparent distaste for all things, and recast it into actual statements of general negativity. Like a giant black hole of "meh," Grumpy Cat gave new voice to the eternally pessimistic. She had become, simply put, the world's perfect "sourpuss."

From general negativity, hoewever, she quickly went from being merely "grumpy" to something darker. Others in pain? Good. Disease and pestilence? Welcome. A national disaster? Makes her day.

Meme-makers had her quickly crossing genres, where symbols of pure evil and despair were no match for her Serene Grumpitude:

I've sometimes wondered though: What accounts for this frowning feline's huge popularity? Perhaps there is some part of our collective world outlook that she taps into, some well of pessimism which many are happy to see has finally been given not only voice but a true champion. She says what the rest of us wish we could.

Part of her allure, of course, is that she is a cat. Domesticated cats already hold in our culture a curiously high and revered status, given that they don't do much of anything but sleep, eat and poop in boxes. While dogs often appear attention-starved, hyperactive and desperate, cats, by contrast, have "attitude." You must *earn* their affection. You will try, and you will fail. Like Galadriel with the One Ring, all would love her and despair.

The rest of her powers, of course, lay in that frown. Like the mysterious smile of the Mona Lisa, Grumpy Cat's mouth has the uncanny quality of saying so much *more*. The viewer wonders, what is she really thinking? What secrets does she hide? And why does she hate us so?

The beauty of it, of course, is that Grumpy Cat is really just that — grumpy. She doesn't *really* hate everything, we just like to think she does. And she isn't really the face of pure evil. That honor may belong elsewhere:

Who Is This Grumpy Cat You Speak Of?

We're as fond of Grumpy Cat's grumpiness as we are of grumpy old people who shout at us to get off their lawns. I'm reminded of Shirley McClaine's character Wheezer in *Steel Magnolias*, who famously quipped that she wasn't a bitch, she'd just been in a bad mood for twenty years. Or Grandpa Gustafson in *Grumpy Old Men* itself, who groused "Kids. Can't live with them, can't shoot them." Even once young and glamorous stars of stage and film maintain their appeal in their golden years by going bitchy on us. As Dolly Parton put it, "I'm old enough now and cranky enough now, that if someone tried to tell me what to do, I'd tell them where to put it."

We adore our cranks for two reasons. First, they say what we all merely think. We septuagenarian-plussers don't care as much what people think of us, so the world gets described without nice filters.

Second, others forgive the grumpiness because the world likes to believe, deep down, that all that piss and vinegar coats a heart of gold.

Case in point: Grumpy Cat became so known for saying "no" that a "yes" from her was considered revolutionary. My own experience was telling. Around the time of the marriage equality court cases in March 2013, I called upon fans to change their profile pictures to a pink equality symbol on a red background. (I devote an entire chapter later in this book to this particular point in our collective online history, which was both surprising in its reach and profoundly impactful.) As the Internet so often does, this symbol began morphing quickly, with all manner of mutations popping up. But one of my favorites simply showed Grumpy Cat, the sultana of shade and the queen of meme herself, holding up a simple sign:

Everyone understood what this conveyed: If

Grumpy Cat could bring herself to actually support something, it should be a no-brainer for mere humans.

At one point, Grumpy Cat and I were up for the same award — the Distinguished Achievement Award for Internet Culture, given out at the Shorty Awards. (I didn't really know what to say when I won this, other than to compare it to another unexpected honor: "Thank you for this award; it's just as cool as having an asteroid named after me.") I expected Grumpy Cat to come after me in light of the besting, but happily for me, she didn't seem particularly phased by the loss. In fact, she recovered well, and apparently is now the official spokescat for Friskies cat food, which itself is the height of irony.

A final aside: Grumpy Cat's real name is Tardar, which is a truncation of a misspelled "Tardar Sauce." She goes by Tard for short, which means her nickname is also a coincidental and unfortunate derogatory vernacular for the mentally handicapped. When I first used "Tard" to describe her in a post, I captioned it with what I believed was a wholly innocent line, "Don't be tard-y to the party."

Many disagreed. The comment feed (and my FB wall) quickly filled up with pleas and cries from special needs advocates, who were anywhere from "saddened" to "shocked and appalled" that I would use a term like "Tard" so cavalierly.

To be honest, it took me a while even to understand what they were talking about. As I would *never* use "retard" to refer to someone with a developmental disability, "tard" was an abbreviation I didn't even know. But try explaining that to a fan. My attempt to note that the cat's *name* was Tardar and that I wasn't belittling her earned me no points with an increasingly unsettled mob. "We don't use retard to describe things we don't like, just as we don't say something is 'so gay' anymore, George. I'm surprised and disappointed to see that you of all people would use a term like 'tard' on your page."

I should mention that many other fans, weary of the language police, leapt to my defense, pointing out that I obviously meant no offense, and was simply trying to make a clumsy pun. But this experience, bizarre as it was, has me now steering clear of controversy and avoiding even any suggestion of the term "retarded." (For the same reasons, I wonder about terms like "crippling" and "niggardly" which have perfectly benign meanings, unrelated to the words they resemble, but in the hands of the linguistically challenged and easily "butt-hurt," cause undue offence.) No matter: henceforth, Tard would simply be "Grumpy Cat."

One final observation: People have been quick

to assume all manner of ills and hatefulness simply based on that look on Grumpy Cat's face. But perhaps she merely has "bitchy resting face," as the site Funny or Die once lampooned. She can't help her outer frown, any more than Simon Cowell can help revealing his inner bitch during terrible auditions on *American Idol.* For much the same reason, we look to them for the honest, unvarnished truth. Perhaps Grumpy Cat hits a nerve precisely because we're all a little grumpy ourselves, but have learned to hide it well. That she doesn't, and can't, may explain our Grumpy Cat obsession. Maybe we're just a "tard" too much like her to admit.

Link Wars

It's no secret that I use Facebook to promote my blog, books and "Takei" merchandise (the obligatory T-shirts, mugs and mousepads that certain fans love to collect) — the money from which is either donated to charity, or used to compensate my staffers, who tirelessly monitor and collect the finest Internet gems. For much of 2012, I was quite open and straightforward about what we were hawking. "My new book is out, and I'd be honored if you picked up a copy." "I've designed a T-shirt for 'straight' supporters to wear — come be part of the TSA — the Takei Straight Alliance." "'It's OK to be Takei' merchandise is now on sale, all proceeds to charity."

Despite this effort to be forthright, I caught a

great deal of flak from fans who thought that *my own* page should contain nothing that isn't there solely to amuse them, and that I shouldn't even make it self-sustaining by, heaven forbid, *selling* anything on it. "Stop with the shameless plugs, George." "This page used to be fun" and "George is just trying to push his book on us."

That last complaint really irks me. After all, other than during the holiday buying season, I probably post 20 funny memes or interesting articles for every one post about my book or merchandise. And even if now and then I do plug my book, is this different from any other "celebrity"? My goodness, if any of these grumblers bothered to so much as take a quick peek at the pages of pop bands, celebrity designers or even certain other *Star Trek* personalities, they would quickly deduce that those pages read like 24/7 infomercials. I've always instructed my team to keep the page quite light on commerce — aiming more for a gentle public radio-like entreaty than an ad-laden platform for self-promotion.

Still, the complaints kept up, and I began to understand how some folks at Facebook itself might feel about their own user base: despite receiving a *free* service that fans are under no obligation to use, many still complained and oozed negativity, indignant to be asked to purchase something from time to time. It's not as if the occasional promotion takes up any of their time. Goodness, no one has ever required them to buy the item in question. Unlike TV or in a movie theater, it is quite simple to ignore or "scroll past" the ads, just as someone who doesn't want to see an ad in a magazine can just turn the page. But still a handful of the most vocal fans continued to gripe.

So I tried a different tack, seeking a more acceptable way to offer my own items on my own page. One idea was to address the matter head-on by admitting that I was doing some shilling. After all, we are all adults here. As a self-published author, who will pitch my book if I don't? Many other fans pointed this out when someone complained. "There's nothing wrong with George talking about his own book on his own page," one wrote. "If you ever write a book and want your friends to buy it, you'd do the same."

Another idea was, of course, to use humor. People are more likely to "forgive" even blatant self-promotion, *if* the script is entertaining enough. (As I observed in an earlier chapter, who doesn't remember Wendy's infamous "Where's the beef?!" ad, which people stuck around to watch just to hear that old woman bark those words? Young'uns, ask your parents.) So I began a series that I called "Shameless Plugs," where I would find images or cartoons of, well, plugs. Here's an example:

I'd say something like , "Here are a couple of truly shameless plugs. Speaking of which, have you ordered your copy of *Oh Myyy?*"

Another read, "Shatner always got my name wrong. It's pronounced 'Takei,' as in, rhymes with 'toupee.' And yes, it's a well-made hairpiece, not obvious plugs. Speaking of which, have you bought my book yet?"

I started running out of creative ways to talk about "plugs," so I went to the next closest thing I could think of:

after which I wrote, "Oh, you said shameless PUGS. Here you go: http://po.st/QCv79Q"

My staffers began to report, however, that despite my efforts to keep things fresh and fun, our book sales were declining, because fewer and fewer people were actually clicking on my links. The problem was this: The links usually quite clearly indicated that they were for a book or a t-shirt or some other sponsored merchandise. In other words, I'd become predictable, and as a consequence it was easy for fans to simply scroll on by.

This phenomenon of ignoring links based on their previews, whether to news articles, funny stories or my merchandise, was steadily growing. I began to suspect that most people looking at a preview link were making split-second decisions not to be taken away from the primary feed. Like people reading newspaper headlines, they skimmed past the substance with the confidence that they already knew what lay on the other side of the link, and thus didn't need to click further. The Internet is indeed so filled with clutter that yet another link with yet another preview photo can get so easily lost in the clamor.

So my staff suggested that, for all the outside links we put on the Facebook page, we ought to remove the preview altogether. This way, if people wanted to know what the link led to, they'd actually have to click on it.

I liked the new, uncluttered link format. It was as if we'd gift-wrapped each link, with just enough of a teaser to whet the curiosity. Fans would have to trust me that I would send them somewhere interesting. And ninety percent of the time, that was to a funny, informative or epic story that a fan or one of my staff had found and forwarded. And yes, about ten percent of the time, it was to my book or merchandise page. I actually thought that was a pretty fair balance, more or less on par with commercials on a TV show. If people didn't want to click the link, they were free to ignore it, just scroll on by.

I also liked knowing I wasn't filling up fans' newsfeeds with large images and text. You see, among the more "vocal" pundits who comment on my Facebooking, a chief criticism is the amount of "Internet noise" I am said to generate, which supposedly pushes "legitimate" news stories out of the way in favor of ridiculous cat videos. I doubt those pundits have actually spent much time on my page, on which I have laboriously included important news stories and thoughtful editorials on everything from the uprisings in Turkey to homelessness to Russia's anti-LGBT laws. Complaining that these links take you on occasion to a cat video is like lamenting the fact that a lot of TV channels are for entertainment, not news.

So in 2013, I went ahead with the unpreviewed links. My team even gave me my own personalized URL abbreviation: http://ohmyyy.gt (Technically, I'm told that the "gt" stands for Guatamala, but you and I both know what it's really for.)

Predictably, a small minority of fans howled at the new format. "This link baiting is beneath you, George," scolded one. "I like having a preview of what I'm about to see," wrote another. Oh dear. Damned if you do, damned if you don't. This was akin to those annoying people in line who demand samples of every flavor of ice cream, before deciding after 10 minutes that they don't like any of them and walking away. I figured, if the fans trust me, they'd know I wouldn't lead them astray.

In terms of click-throughs, my staffers were right. Giving just a hint, but not a full description, of where each link led increased clicks on average by 200 percent. Many of these links were important articles which needed to be read in their entirety, and not merely skimmed in previews, so I was happy to see that rise. It also meant greater general engagement by fans which, as I discussed in my previous book, in turn meant greater likelihood that the status would be "favored" by Facebook and thus more likely to be streamed into fans' newsfeeds.

Facebook became wise, however, to this kind of blind-linking. Soon, it began to issue warnings to users that they were being taken away from Facebook, and that Facebook couldn't vouch for the security of the site they were being led to. That seemed unnecessarily alarmist to me. Fans complained that they were receiving this message, but again I figured if people trusted me, they knew I wouldn't lead them to a site that would spam them or phish for personal information. Still, the ploy by Facebook worked, and we saw a drop of engagement from fans on our "blind link" strategy whenever that message popped up.

Speaking of "engagement," I also decided that if I was going to ask fans to look at my book or merchandise page, I might as well make the process a bit more fun. So in the spirit of gaming, I often included a puzzle, riddle or mind bender with my promotional posts.

And by this I don't mean the utterly banal types of polls or "puzzles" that are solely intended to score as many Facebook "likes" as possible (a scam called "like farming" that mines for users and then sells the page to another company). We've all seen those, where they show you an interesting picture and ask you to type "1" in the comments to see what happens next:

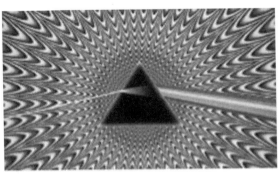

"Type 1 in the comments to see what happens!"

Of course, Facebook doesn't permit .gif files (graphic interchange format for you non-techies), so of course nothing "happens next", but you can now be included in a list of dupes who typed 1 and have your user name sold to the highest bidder.

Or those so-called "puzzles" that set a stupidly low bar for users:

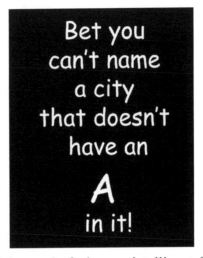

To think people feel more intelligent for having come up with one is rather depressing. Even more depressing is the unbridled use of comic sans.

Then there are the polls that are simply annoying:

I'm not even sure why people bother participating

in this, but many hundreds of thousands will gladly like and share away on the PB&J poll. (By the way, peanut butter was in the lead, last I checked.)

No, my own puzzles, I vowed, would be more interesting. One of my favorites was this:

> **LOOK VERY CLOSELY. CAN YOU FIND THE**
> **THE MISTAKE?**
>
> **0 1 2 3 4 5 6 7 8 9**
> **IF YOU CAN, THEN YOU'RE PROBABLY BRIGHT ENOUGH TO**
> **APPRECIATE THIS:**

(at which point, I'd add a link to my book.) The advantage of this kind of post was obvious. My fans love games as much as I do, and while no one wants to share an advertisement for a book, sharing a particularly clever mind-teaser with their friends is a totally different ball of wax. And if that mind-teaser "happened" to contain a link to my book, somehow it seemed less objectionable that way. Voila! Viral marketing at its finest.

Another puzzle asked,

> **HOW MANY FS DO YOU COUNT IN THE FOLLOWING:**
>
> **FINISHED FILES ARE THE RE-**
> **SULT OF YEARS OF SCIENTIF-**
> **IC STUDY COMBINED WITH**
> **THE EXPERIENCE OF YEARS.**
>
> **MANY PEOPLE MISS THAT THERE ARE IN FACT SIX FS. BUT**
> **IF YOU COUNTED FOUR OR MORE, YOU'RE CERTAINLY BRIGHT**
> **ENOUGH TO APPRECIATE THIS:**

...and another book link. Truly, I've found that people don't mind taking a gander at the link if you give them something to play with first. After several of these types of promotions, one fan commented good-naturedly, "Dammit, Takei! You get me to click that link every time!"

Lately fans have caught on and started sending me some very funny pictogram puzzles. I use these to see if people "get" the joke right away, and if they do, encourage them to read my book for more, or reward themselves with a "Takei Friendly" T-shirt (proceeds from those sales to charity). Here's an example:

This unfortunately seemed to sail over the heads

of anyone who didn't come of age by the 1980s. So I tried something simpler:

Photo Credit - Jaco Haasbroek (jacohaasbroek.com)

For this many fans gleefully liked the post and clicked through to my Takei Friendly T-shirt. I received no complaints from fans that I was "promoting" my merchandise again, because at the very least I had entertained them in the process. I did receive complaints, however, from fans who believed that one was too easy. So I threw one up for the brainy nerds:

You might be wondering, aren't I worried that we're giving away all our marketing secrets? Eh, not really. If others wind up copying the way my team and I run the Facebook page, it's not the end of the world. We still have the luxury of having a comfortable head start in absolute fan numbers and engagement, and honestly, even though I've gotten many of them to click through to my book, most of the five million+ fans of my page (as of press time) aren't going to be reading this book anyway. If they were, I'd be very rich indeed. So, copy away. It will keep my staff on their toes to come up with new and innovative ways to both entertain and be self-sustaining. And anyway, as they will say in the distant future, "Replication is the sincerest form of flattery."

Dogged Determination

It is a truth universally acknowledged that *cats* rule the Internet, and that dogs come in a distant second. This comes as no surprise, given the material that tends to gain instant net virality and popularity. "Epic fails," for example, are only worth watching if the subject appears poised and capable, before accidentally stepping off a table, setting herself on fire, or slipping humiliatingly into some body of water. When you think about it, watching a dog fall into a bathtub isn't nearly as funny as watching a cat do it. (I should note here, however, that one of the funniest videos I have ever seen features a rascal of a dog pushing a cat, quite purposefully, into a bathtub. You can view it here: http://po.st/yYPwRI)

A dog falling in a tub isn't funny because we have come to expect dogs to be good-naturedly clumsy, less-than-perfect, and emotionally transparent. When a dog falls into water, it doesn't pretend it *meant* to do it. Instead, the dog will simply sit there, tongue out, sopping wet, enjoying the sudden change of circumstance, with an expression that says, "Hey, that was fun! Let's do it again!" The wet cat, on the other hand, will either be simultaneously mortified and angry at *you* for witnessing it or, as mentioned, will act like that was her plan all along.

It's pretty much the same with dogs and cars. A dog will find a ride in any motorized vehicle (so long as it's not to the V-E-T) a simply amazing experience, no matter how many times he's done it before. Even the mere utterance of the words "car" or "ride" might result in a dog sitting upright and alert, eye upon the door, ready for its great adventure. Most dogs need no urging to climb in and, once inside, will stare eagerly, back and forth between you and the window, until with a sigh you roll it down. Very few dogs can resist the sheer joy of feeling the wind on their faces, the world rushing by.

Nerds might remember that it was a dog, Laika (a stray mutt from the streets of Moscow), that was the first animal to enter outer space and to orbit the Earth as a passenger onboard the Soviet satellite Sputnik

2. Laika proved that animals could survive the initial rigors of space travel, including the G-forces involved in blast-off. Sadly, within a few hours of her departure from Earth, the vessel transporting her overheated and Laika perished from the heat—a grisly fact only made public long after the fall of the Communist Party.

But in the future, when dogs do travel safely in space at warp speed with their humans, be assured they will still try to stick their heads out of starship vessels, as photographer Benjamin "The Frogman" Grelle has captured so perfectly:

If you're thinking, as I did, "This is totally photo-shopped," it may be the stars zipping past that give it away. (For more great photos by Grelle, visit www. thefrogman.me)

By contrast, the common car ride is far less enjoyable for cats, as any cat-person will attest. Best to place the cat first in a carrier, and ensure it is mildly to heavily sedated. To a cat, the notion that its body can move at such speeds without any conscious effort by said cat can produce near apoplexy. It may also cause serious injury to passengers or the driver, as the cat attempts at all cost to escape its inevitable demise. It can even lead to an embarrassing loss of bladder or bowel control—by the cat and sometimes the driver.

In fairness, dogs aren't above their own sense of horror, dismay or sadness. There are moving and well-documented stories of dogs who have stood vigil by their humans' graves, neither eating nor moving, so strong is their grief. There are videos of dogs so overcome by the sight of their humans coming home after a long war that the dog appears crying with joy.

Then there are the priceless facial expressions, which the Internet has captured on occasion. Some dogs, for example, enjoy watching television with their owners. It hasn't always been clear whether the dog actually understands any of what it sees, or that what appears in the magic box isn't real. After all, the people in the box have no smell (and more specifically, have no butts to sniff), so they must not be *completely* real. No matter—here, "Buddy" seems to believe what he is watching all too well.

On reflection, allowing Buddy to watch the end of Old Yeller may not have been the best idea.

Certain breeds of dogs seem always to have the *same* expressions. It was pointed out to me, for example, that even on the happiest occasions, pugs always look like they have forgotten something important, like whether they turned off the oven.

In fairness, other animals have certain kinds of

permanent looks about them. For example, another fan pointed out that eels maintain a very cartoonish appearance that, once described, is quite spot-on:

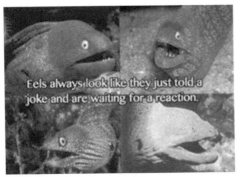

Eels always look like they just told a joke and are waiting for a reaction.

Hah? HAH?! (Which reminds me of an absolutely awful earworm: "When you're diving at night and your feet feel a bite, that's a moray!")

But back to dogs. Humans love to speak to their dogs in the most curious fashion, often with their jaws pushed forward so that their words sound almost dog-like. It's as if somehow the dog will understand us better if our diction is more like theirs (or what we imagine theirs to be). Oddly, this cooing does seem to work, for the tail starts a-waggin' and a-thumpin' soon after the age-old question is posed: "Whoos a goo' boy? Huh? Whoos a goo' boy?" Never mind that this might cause significant existential anxiety:

Puppies are an a category apart, eliciting from the Internet a reaction reserved only for human babies, koalas and pandas—all with the uncanny ability to elicit a collective "awwww." Note that each of these tends to be somewhat roly-poly, move rather slowly, and sleep a great deal (I dare say we all wish we could do this more often). Unsurprisingly, one of my most "liked" and "shared" posts in the early days of my Facebook page involved a picture of a baby surrounded by French bulldog puppies, with no caption by me other than "I'm going to leave this right here for you."

There is something about the innocent sweetness of the baby (which we all know will end by the time she learns the word "mine" at age two) paired with the cuteness overload of puppies (which we know will never lose their genuine affection for that child, even as she grows into that tyrannical two-year old) that touches us all. It probably doesn't hurt that they are all about the same size and rest together without a care in the world. The flush on baby's cheek mirrors the puppies' spots, suggesting that maybe the puppies simply think she is one of them. Can most of us even remember a time when we felt so safe, warm and cuddled?

When it comes down to it, "dog people" indeed love their pets because they are relatively easy to please and eager to show their affection and appreciation. The writers of the movie *Up* made this point in their brilliant use of the translating collar, which confirmed all of our fondest beliefs of the inner workings of a dog's mind. For the most part, dogs simply adore their humans and will do anything for us. They believe that we are better than we are, making us *want* to be our best selves.

Cats, on the other hand, already know we are flawed, and sniff condescendingly, almost pityingly, as they deign to allow us to tend to them. This reminds me of the old joke about the dog and the cat, which have been left on their own for a weekend. "Do you miss the family? I miss the family! Do you miss the family?" the dogs whines. "The family," says the cat, through its teeth, "are the help."

Dogs do not judge us for our failings; rather, they stick by us through thick and thin, loyal to the core.

Whose heart doesn't feel a little tingle and a tug when we see a dog willing to starve beside its homeless owner on the street? (But on that note, isn't it curious that not nearly as many of us equally pity and empathize with the human in this situation? We're so quick to assume that the dog is helpless here, while the human somehow deserves his or her lot. As Spock might say, "Fascinating. And illogical.")

The difference between the dog's breathless and inexhaustible excitement over life and the cat's typically blasé attitude toward it was best captured by a famous meme comparing the two in diary form:

Dog's Diary

8:00 am - Dog food! My favorite thing!

9:30 am - A car ride! My favorite thing!

9:40 am - A walk in the park! My favorite thing!

10:30 am - Got rubbed and petted! My favorite thing!

12:00 pm - Lunch! My favorite thing!

1:00 pm - Played in the yard! My favorite thing!

3:00 pm - Wagged my tail! My favorite thing!

5:00 pm - Milk bones! My favorite thing!

7:00 pm - Got to play ball! My favorite thing!

8:00 pm - Wow! Watched TV with the people! My favorite thing!

11:00 pm - Sleeping on the bed! My favorite thing!

Cat's Diary

Day 983 of my captivity. My captors continue to taunt me with bizarre little dangling objects. They dine lavishly on fresh meat, while the other inmates and I are fed hash or some sort of dry nuggets. Although I make my contempt for the rations perfectly clear, I nevertheless must eat something in order to keep up my strength.

The only thing that keeps me going is my dream of escape. In an attempt to disgust them, I once again vomit on the carpet. Today I decapitated a mouse and dropped its headless body at their feet. I had hoped this would strike fear into their hearts, since it clearly demonstrates what I am capable of. However, they merely made condescending comments about what a 'good little hunter' I am. Fools.

There was some sort of assembly of their accomplices tonight. I was placed in solitary confinement for the duration of the event. However, I could hear the noises and smell the food. I overheard that my confinement was due to the power of 'allergies'. I must learn what this means and how to use it to my advantage...

Today I was almost successful in an attempt to assassinate one of my tormentors by weaving around his feet as he was walking. I must try this again tomorrow -- but at the top of the stairs.

I am convinced that the other prisoners here are flunkies and snitches. The dog receives special privileges. He is regularly released - and seems to be more than willing to return. He is obviously stupid.

The bird has got to be an informant. I observe him communicating with the guards regularly. I am certain that he reports my every move. My captors have arranged protective custody for him in an elevated cell, so he is safe...for now.

If you are reading this on a Kindle and your eyes cannot forgive the size of the cat meme, try clicking on it to expand. It's a little trick I learned in Starfleet Academy.

There are many things that I love about this meme, not the least of which are the difference in font, the structure of the prose, and the un- versus highly- selective use of exclamation points between the two. As this meme suggests, humans assume, with a decent amount of evidence to support the theory, that a dog's memory is rather short-term, its mind ready to be reset by the next exterior stimulus. A cat, by contrast, ponders, remembers, and does not forget, will not forgive.

Many fans on Facebook and Twitter don't realize that Brad and I not only raise cats but are also dog lovers. Our own dog was named "La Reine Blanche," meaning literally "The White Queen" (we called her "Ren-Ren" for short). Now, "La Reine Blanche" might have been a very, shall we say, precious name for a dog. More than a few fans pointed out that by naming her that, I had essentially come out of the closet long before 2005.

La Reine was a breed known as a Papillon, which

means "butterfly" in French. She was regal, beautiful and imperious. Her long, white, silky fur was like a royal cloak. But from her eyes to her widespread butterfly ears, her fur was the color of coffee brushed with rich, dark chocolate. La Reine knew that Brad and I were around solely to serve her slightest whims. She could also be playful, energetic and demanding.

Her favorite toy was a little plastic ring that she loved to have us throw across the back lawn. She would chase after it with her magnificent butterfly ears flying behind her like Isadora Duncan's scarf. Once, we took her to the park to let her chase her ring in the open space of the great lawn. The other dogs playing there were all about her size—miniature poodles, whippets and Scottish terriers. Ren-Ren clearly preferred playing with them. She dropped her ring and romped among her newfound doggy friends nipping and yelping in joy.

But that lasted just so long. She wanted to chase her ring. So I took it and threw it high and long to the far side of the great lawn. Ren-Ren was off and running, her eyes fixed on the ring flying through the air. It landed right near a shaggy wolfhound that had been gamboling with other dogs its size. Ren-Ren came to a skidding stop, made an immediate U-turn, and began racing back toward me with the giant wolfhound bounding after her.

Ren-Ren knew when she was out-sized. She seemed to be flying through the air. I had never seen her run so fast. As she neared me, she leaped up, flying right into my outstretched arms. She was home safe in my embrace.

The wolfhound loped up wagging its tail. It wanted to play. But La Reine wasn't having any of that. She snarled aggressively at the massive menace. And when the wolfhound didn't back off, she began yapping at it, as if protecting me from danger. When the hulk of a dog finally got the message and ambled off, she turned about to lick my face happily. I wasn't sure whether it was in gratitude or to reassure me that *I* was safe, that she had saved *me* from a horrible attack. Ren-Ren was once again reigning from the safety of my arms.

It is a wonderful memory of a special moment with her. We miss her terribly.

George with La Reine Blanche
August 8, 1991, to November 23, 2000, R.I.P.

Pink is the New Black

2013 was a watershed year for LGBT civil rights. The battles were fought town by town, state by state, and at the federal level — but much of the most important public discourse occurred rather broadly...on the Internet. As the popularity of sites like YouTube and Facebook grew, being "out" meant more than making an announcement and introducing family, friends and co-workers to your partner. It meant living out your "gaily life" online, for "friends of friends" or even complete strangers to witness. For the first time, as LGBT issues were debated across newsfeeds and comment streams, netizens could see, gauge and engage with others on important social questions, such as what role, if any, religious beliefs should play in shaping the law, whether traditional marriage was still exclusionary if LGBT couples could separately form "civil unions" with similar legal rights, and whether in a democracy the voting public should be able to decide questions of civil rights by way of referendum.

The Internet, and social media in particular, ensured that nearly everyone knew and was "friends" with at least one gay or lesbian person — at least on Facebook. And here was the shocker: Straight people could experience for the first time that the lives of gays and lesbians pretty much resembled everyone else's. That is to say, aside from the occasional "festive" photos at Pride parades, the "great gay agenda" appeared to comprise the same rather mundane matters that people, straight and gay alike, insist on posting about: "Ate an apple for breakfast," "I lost my car keys," "My children drive me crazy," "Legs Day at the gym."

I cannot overstate the importance that the lifting of the rainbow veil has had on public perception, particularly among younger people for whom sexual orientation gets a "so what" shrug, akin to ethnic origin or religion — a difference where distinction is solely a function of how big a deal others make of it. This was the quiet revolution brewing across millions of computers and mobile devices, spreading almost unnoticed across social media to all aspects of our society, even while the keepers of "traditional" marriage and the proponents of marriage equality prepared to do epic battle in our courts.

Toward the end of March 2013, all eyes turned to the U.S. Supreme Court as it heard two landmark cases, both of which, it so happens, had a deep impact on Brad and me as a couple. I also laced up my boxing gloves and entered the public arena on this issue, ready to engage my increasingly broad base of fans on Facebook and Twitter to raise public awareness over what was at stake.

After all, as I discussed in *Oh Myyy (There Goes the Internet)*, this was a core reason I had begun my online exploits in the first place. I had set out in 2011, initially just on Twitter, with a clear intent to use "funnies" as a kind of sweet honey to attract fans, so that when I actually had something more serious to say, such as on matters of LGBT equality and other issues dear to my heart, I'd have a captive audience. I've never tried to hide my own agenda here. Like a pesky relative at the holidays, your "Uncle George" will be tireless in trying to get you to laugh, but you may have to listen to a few of his opinions over a glass of sherry.

Before I get into what transpired, and how truly groundbreaking and amazing some of the developments in our long battle for equality were, let me give you some background on this pair of lawsuits.

The first case was a challenge to DOMA — the Defense of Marriage Act — a law passed in 1996 that forbade the U.S. government from recognizing the legality of any marriage not between a man and a woman. It also gave states, which would otherwise be required to give "full faith and credit" to marriages performed in other states, the right to refuse to recognize *same-sex* marriages. DOMA had been passed with veto-proof majorities during a climate of backlash against perceived LGBT gains in certain more progressive states, where brave courts and legislators had begun to argue that same-sex couples deserved equal treatment under the law, including legal recognition of their marriages. DOMA set in stone, for the next 17 years, the kind of invidious discrimination that, I am certain, will be looked back upon with distaste and disbelief by future generations.

Defenders of so-called "traditional" marriage often balk when I make the comparison between their beliefs and those of the folks who defended the anti-miscegenation laws that, last century, prevented non-whites from marrying whites. But the similarities are too striking to dismiss. At their heart, anti-miscegenation laws were based on emotional appeals to the "natural" order, much like what we hear today in arguments against same-sex marriage. When the U.S. Supreme Court overturned such laws nationwide in 1967 (yes, less than 50 years ago), in the famous case of *Loving v. Virginia*, the lower court judge in Virginia had this to say about why, in his view, such laws were needed:

> "ALMIGHTY GOD CREATED THE RACES WHITE, BLACK, YELLOW, MALAY, AND RED, AND PLACED THEM ON SEPARATE CONTINENTS, AND BUT FOR THE INTERFERENCE WITH HIS ARRANGEMENT THERE WOULD BE NO CAUSE FOR SUCH MARRIAGES. THE FACT THAT HE SEPARATED THE RACES SHOWS THAT HE DID NOT INTEND THE RACES TO MIX."

In overturning these laws, the U.S. Supreme Court held that there was a fundamental right to marry implicit within the Constitution, which protected the individual and individual rights in the face of government intrusion. The state of Virginia argued that the law merely reflected the existing and real prejudices of the citizenry, and was merely trying to help interracial couples avoid that prejudice. How magnanimous of them. In other words, Virginia argued public disapproval would harm the couple more than denying their right to get married in the first place. The Supreme Court rightfully ruled that this logic would in effect enshrine such prejudice forever into the law, and that mere animus or social disapproval was not a sufficient basis for the passing of such laws, especially when the individual personal stakes (here, the right to marry the person you love) are so high.

DOMA did basically the same thing the Virginia law had done decades before. Based on lawmakers' disapproval and personal distaste for homosexuality, DOMA legalized marriage discrimination based on a couple's sexual orientation. It imparted the cold, unmistakable sting of officially-sanctioned prejudice and delivered the devastating and unmistakable message to same-sex couples and their families that they did not exist in the eyes of the law.

But DOMA also had real financial consequences. Many people are unaware that federal law grants 1,138 rights and privileges to married couples, including tax breaks, inheritance tax waivers, medical leave, and hospital visitation rights. By denying those same rights to same-sex married couples, DOMA created two classes of married citizens — those entitled to all those rights and privileges, and those who were not. That alone to me and many others seems downright *un*-American.

Enter Edie Windsor, an 85-year old woman who

121

had been legally married to her spouse Thea Spyer in the state of New York. Edie and Thea had been together 44 years, and when Thea passed away, she left her half of the estate to Edie. Now, normally, there is a federal tax exemption for surviving spouses. The government isn't so callous as to levy a "death" tax upon a widow right after the person with whom she shared her whole life has passed. That would be cruel, indeed. But the rule didn't apply to a *lesbian* widow who had lost her spouse. In Edie's case, because under Section 3 of DOMA the federal government didn't recognize her marriage, she was slapped with a tax on the transfer — to the tune of over $363,000 — to add to her grief. In short, the IRS forced Edie to pay this tax because her marriage, while legal in New York, was not legal as far as Uncle Sam was concerned. As Edie put it, it was as if the U.S. government had treated her and Thea like they were strangers.

Now, Americans are not a tax-loving people; our very independence arose because, as colonies of the British crown, we were being taxed with absolutely no say-so in the matter. It was *taxation without representation*. In this case, for one little old lady, this was *taxation with discrimination*, and she was having none of it. She filed suit to overturn Section 3 of DOMA. A more perfect plaintiff to challenge the injustices and inequities of DOMA could hardly have been imagined.

Brad and I had the good fortune of meeting Edie
shortly after the U.S. Supreme Court ruling.

The second case was a challenge to California's Proposition 8, which sought to amend the California Constitution to define marriage as only between a man and a woman. The history of same-sex marriage in California requires a bit of explanation and, frankly, some untangling. In 2005, both chambers of the Democrat-controlled legislature passed a bill that, for the first time, equalized the status of same-sex couples who sought to be legally married. That bill was, to our dismay, vetoed by Governor Schwarzenegger despite previous assurances that he would treat gays and lesbians equally. But in 2006, the mayor of San Francisco, Gavin Newsom, bravely challenged state law by instructing clerks to begin issuing marriage

123

licenses without regard to the gender or orientation of the parties. Thousands of LGBT couples lined up to be married as City Hall erupted in spontaneous celebrations, putting a very human face to the second-class marital status the couples had so long endured. The San Francisco Clerk's office was open round the clock to meet the crush of demand for marriage licenses. The licenses, however, had not yet been amended to fit the new reality, as they still specified "bride" and "groom," leading to some amusing debates by the giddy couples as to who should be listed in each spot.

A court challenge from conservative political groups to San Francisco's same-sex marriages led to a preliminary halt to further licenses being issued until the constitutionality of California's marriage law (which still defined marriage as solely between a man and a woman) could be reviewed by the courts. For two years, the matter wound its way through the state court system until, in 2008, in a landmark ruling, the California Supreme Court sided with proponents of same-sex marriage, holding that the California Constitution's guarantees of equal treatment under the law required the issuance of marriage licenses without regard to sexual orientation or the gender make-up of the couples.

It was a glorious time. Brad and I, along with

18,000 other couples, were married in 2008 under the laws of California, as interpreted by our state Supreme Court. But our opponents, having lost their legal battle at the highest state court level, weren't going to relinquish the keys to their club that easily. They switched tactics and now turned to the court of public opinion with Proposition 8, which sought to amend the California Constitution to define marriage as only between a man and a woman. It was particularly distressing to see that religious organizations from outside California, particularly the Mormon Church based in Utah, were pumping millions of dollars into Proposition 8 so that marriages such as mine and Brad's would never be legitimate under the law. There is something potently ironic that the Mormon Church, which for decades permitted and even encouraged polygamy, would have anything to say on the matter of "traditional" marriage.

It is also hard to describe how it feels to know that your rights, your marriage and your love are about to be *voted* upon by others, as if the majority has some right to tell you what your heart is allowed to feel or your mind is allowed to think. Normally, we think of our rights as inalienable, such as the right to religion and freedom of speech, the right to a jury trial or the right to an attorney. These are rights we all share, because we are governed by the same laws and should be equal in its eyes. These aren't some transient rights that might disappear if put to a vote. Imagine waking up to hear that your rights to worship, or assemble, or live your life with the person you choose was going to be put to a vote, and if half the people didn't vote your way, "Hasta la vista, rights." These basic rights aren't supposed to be vulnerable. They are part of our guaranteed freedoms.

I have some perspective on this. When I was a small child growing up in Los Angeles, my family was forced from our home by soldiers with bayonetted rifles, simply because we happened to look like the people who had bombed Pearl Harbor. Our rights to a fair trial and to due process were stripped away by President Roosevelt with a single proclamation, and national security as a justification. We weren't charged with anything, let alone convicted of any crimes, but 120,000 of us, most of us American citizens, were forced to live behind barbed wire and armed guards in ten U.S. concentration camps, for no other reason than that we were of Japanese descent.

As my father once explained to me, our "rights" are only as strong as the democracy that protects them. Because we are a people's democracy here in America, as great as the people of this country can be, but also as fallible, we must stay ever vigilant in the face of any "tyranny" of the majority, no mat-

126

ter the stated objective. The Presidential Election of 2008 was therefore a bittersweet moment for many of us in California, who saw such hope in a country where the first black president could be elected just 140 some years after slavery itself was abolished, yet where the rights of millions of LGBT people could be voted away by a nervous, fearful majority.

And so it was now our turn to take our case back to the courts, to argue that amending a state's constitution to enshrine an inequality was anathema to equal protection itself. It would take five more long years, where my own marriage was literally in legal limbo, before the case would find its way to the U.S. Supreme Court, paired with the DOMA case, which everyone knew would have historic and sweeping effect no matter how the Court ruled.

It was in this climate of uncertainty, excitement and change that we found ourselves near the end of March of 2013, when the cases were heard, at last, by the nine justices. Many placed great hope upon the key swing vote of the court, Justice Anthony Kennedy, who had broken twice before from his conservative base to vote with his liberal colleagues on the question of LGBT rights, in one instance invalidating Colorado's Amendment 2 (which kept any municipality in the state from passing LGBT non-discrimination ordinances) and in another striking down

127

Texas's anti-gay sodomy statute as unconstitutional, overturning two decades of laws that had permitted the criminalization of the act of love between two people of the same sex.

As the day approached, certainly none of the justices could escape the conclusion that the pair of decisions would be historic — and that therefore perhaps *history* ultimately would be the judge of their decision. We all hoped Justice Kennedy, in particular, understood where history was headed. Poll after poll showed that, while the American public overall was fairly evenly split on the question of same-sex marriage, *young* people (meaning folks under 40, who seem *quite* young to me) favored it by large majorities, while older Americans opposed it. This was an unmistakable trend, indeed probably irreversible, and, therefore, it really was only a matter of time before the laws would change organically if the Court did not invalidate them now.

Same Sex Marriage: Public Polls since 1988

Now, the Supreme Court is supposed to be above the sway of public opinion and the ever-changing tides in the culture wars. But the justices often listen to the counsel of their clerks, or are at least cognizant of the personal views of court staff or even their own family members. Many of the people around them, therefore, were part of a generation where same-sex marriage bans feel like the last vestiges of an era of intolerance and ignorance. And so while the justices themselves may not be active on social media, where these opinions were voiced daily, no doubt many who influenced them personally were.

I saw an opportunity to use the occasion of the marriage equality case hearings, as well as the phenomenon of social media, to help drive home the inevitability of same-sex marriage. I had learned that the Human Rights Campaign was running a program leading up to the hearings, in which Facebook users were asked to change their profile pictures to a pink and red version of the HRC "equal sign" logo. While the idea was a good one, there hadn't been a large enough online response to create sufficient momentum for the campaign. A few hundred or even a few thousand profile changes would make little impression. I knew that, when it came to such an emotional issue and historic moment, three things would have to happen.

First, there would have to be a strong personal connection between Facebook users and the campaign organizers to have any impact. Having an organization, no matter how worthy or well-intentioned, as the sole rallying point would never work. It's easier to let down a faceless organization than a friend or person you see regularly. Second, we would need to find a way to enlist the help of not just LGBTs, but our straight allies as well. We would have to get the word out to them, and they would need a compelling and *personal* reason to change their profiles in support. And third, for this to work it would truly have to "tip" and become a phenomenon. Like the doomed French students at the barricades, unless the people rose up in support, the cause would be lost.

So when I made the decision to change my own profile picture to the "pinkified" HRC logo, I decided I would use up some social capital and make a direct plea to fans to do the same. Now, I knew that my LGBT fanbase were ready to make the switch in a heartbeat. But how to get millions of straight fans to do likewise?

I read somewhere that the number one reason people have a change of heart for the better on LGBT issues is actually *knowing and interacting* with a gay or lesbian person. This is the power of "coming out" — not only does it provide a positive example to those still fearful that they will be alone after taking that step, it dispels commonly held stereotypes among ordinary citizens about the way LGBT people really are, especially in our own ordinary lives. It is even more powerful when a family member or friend comes out, because others must confront, perhaps for the first time, where they even stand on the question of LGBT equality. After all, denying someone a basic right takes on a whole different cast when it is YOUR CHILD who would be excluded. Will things change? Will there be rejection or acceptance? And how will they talk to others about their gay friend or family member?

And so I thought: Here I am, an openly gay man, who has for some reason become part of the daily life of millions of fans mostly by posting a bunch of silly cat and sci-fi memes. But whatever the reason, I was an LGBT person with whom many straight people felt a unique personal connection. And I was one of the few who was fortunate enough in California to get married to my long-time partner Brad before Proposition 8 threw our status into doubt. And so I asked my fans, both gay and straight, to change their profiles in support. And when I did so, I reminded them of this: The next time same-sex marriage comes up, remember that you do know a gay married couple, George and Brad Takei. Do we not deserve love? Doesn't our love deserve to be recognized?

It was this personal touch that made the difference. To my astonishment, hundreds of thousands of fans followed my lead, setting off a wave of change across Facebook. It was amazing to watch a tide of pink gather and form, with our straight allies making up so much of our force. I couldn't have imagined a stronger virtual showing. For a few glorious days, everywhere I looked I saw those two equality bars in pink, each saying "I'm a supporter of love and equality." It was our own "March on Washington," and we had indeed overcome. By the end of the tide, millions had followed suit, and Facebook was awash with pink.

Online antics being what they are, the Equality Symbol began to morph as users laid claim to or included various genres, symbols and icons. One of my favorites, naturally, arose from the sci-fi community and appropriated the rallying cry of a beleaguered human race on the run, as portrayed in *Battlestar Galactica*:

Other sci-fi fans soon weighed in. The vampire lovers (thankfully, fans of the real ones, not the sparkly sort) had their fun, too. With vampire rights and gay rights so brilliantly analogized by the popular series *True Blood* (even to the point where opponents carried signs reading "God Hates Fangs"), this was an easy fit:

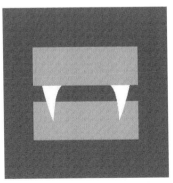

Bacon lovers also had their say, as they always do with anything that even remotely resembles bacon, whether it be road signs or equality signs:

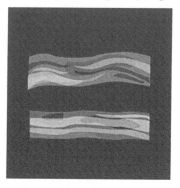

And not to be outdone, butter lovers rallied with their own emblem, playing off the then-popular and now-somewhat-disgraced Southern personality, Paula Deen:

People wondered whether, as a gay man, I was in any way offended by these posts. Not one tiny bit. For me, those heady days were a raucous celebration of diversity and humanity, the best kind of spontaneous outpouring. And so anyone who wanted to join, however they wanted, was welcome to it.

The equality symbol apparently has legs. In the late summer of 2013, the CEO of the pasta company Barilla was embroiled in one of the biggest PR controversies in recent corporate memory by going on a radio show in Italy and stating that his company would certainly not be showing gay families in their advertising, and that if gay people had a problem with that, they could eat another kind of pasta. Now, if there's anything companies should have learned in 2013, it's how *not* to piss off groups of people or communities who are incredibly tight on social media. Within minutes of this statement, it was all over Facebook: Dump Barilla. Links to the translations of the radio interview immediately popped up on popular LGBT blogs; angry queens (who didn't want the carbs anyway) snapped Instagrams of their garbage cans filled with Barilla pasta; mock-ups of Barilla boxes with "Bigotoni" pasta flashed up on Pinterest and Tumblr; and then this profile pic resurfaced:

Just. Brilliant.

But back to March and the Supreme Court. After the hearings were over, we and the rest of America waited, and waited…and waited. We knew that the marriage equality cases would probably be the last ones announced in the session because the Court prefers to leave the most important decisions for the very end, in part because their importance means the hubbub around them would drown out anything announced afterwards, and in part because the justices probably don't want protestors near the Courthouse for the remainder of the term.

So uncertain was the outcome that I actually prepared three different status updates for my Facebook page — one which celebrated, another which expressed satisfaction with some reservations, and another which excoriated the Court. Happily, it was the first of these that I joyously posted, praising Justice

Anthony Kennedy for joining again with his socially liberal colleagues in a 5-4 decision striking down DOMA, and marveling that I had lived to see the day when marriage equality was recognized by the federal government, 44 years after the Stonewall riots began the LGBT civil rights movement in 1969.

Edie Windsor became an instant hero to us all, her name forever associated with the case that ended official discrimination against gay and lesbian couples on the federal books. The decision, *Windsor v. United States*, struck down Section 3 of DOMA and required the IRS to repay Edie the money it had levied as taxes on her wife's estate. Now, to no one's surprise, a host of other questions immediately emerged around immigration and naturalization rights, health benefits and all of the financial benefits and privileges enjoyed by straight married couples. The government and its various agencies are busily sorting all of this out, and I am confident it will all be ironed out fairly.

As expected, Prop 8 was tossed out on a technicality. It turned out, since the Attorney General and Governor of California had refused to enforce Prop 8, or appeal the ruling by the District Court striking it down, no one had any real "standing" to continue to appeal the case up the chain to the Supreme Court. That meant that the District Court's decision stood, and that marriages were free to resume in California.

It wasn't a decision, therefore, "on the merits," but for those of us who had been in limbo all this time, it was a win. Prop 8 was done, marriage equality was once again the law of the state.

Indeed, since the DOMA ruling, one by one states have been passing marriage equality in their legislatures, or state supreme courts have ordered the government to issue marriage licenses to same-sex couples. As I write this, that number this very day has risen now to 17, as the New Mexico Supreme Court has just issued a unanimous ruling that expands marriage equality to all its citizens, including same-sex spouses. A map of America reveals what you might expect — that the more liberal New England and West Coast states, with a scattering of "blue" states in the Midwest like Illinois and Iowa, have taken this step.

But I caution that LGBT equality is not—and should not be—a partisan issue, even though it is often treated as such. Some of the staunchest supporters of our rights happen to be arch-conservatives, including for example the late Senator Barry Goldwater, who was among the first in Washington to endorse a law protecting LGBTs from discrimination in the workplace. Also from the state of Arizona is Senator (and former presidential nominee) John McCain, who recently voted "Yea" on the passage of the Employment Non-Discrimination Act, along with Senator Rob Portman from Ohio, a staunch conservative. It bears noting that Messrs. Goldwater, McCain and Portman share something in common—a beloved family member who came out. In Goldwater's case, it was his grandson; in McCain's case, it was his daughter; in Portman's case, it was his son. This demonstrates to me that fair-minded people of good conscience cannot help but be moved by the personal experience of knowing someone they love is gay or lesbian. It makes a difference. It lifts that "rainbow veil."

As an astonishing symbol of how much things have changed, the week before I wrote these words I saw an article on the first same-sex wedding performed at Westpoint. This struck me deeply. I had recently been asked to write a forward for the book, *Soldier of Change: From the Closet to the Forefront of the Gay Rights Movement* by Stephen Snyder-Hill. You might recall, during the Republican primaries in September of 2011, Stephen had the courage to say he was a gay solider serving in Iraq and wanted to know whether the candidates would allow soldiers to continue to serve openly without fear of losing their jobs. For this question, he shockingly was *booed* by the audience, and Senator Rick Santorum went on to respond that he stood opposed to the "social experimentation" going on in the military, and that as President he would reinstate "Don't Ask, Don't Tell" because "sex has no place in the military."

But it's now two years later, and we've come so far that there simply is no going back. And why would we want to, when there is so much love, acceptance and promise ahead?

A group of California children were recently asked to watch two viral videos of marriage proposals, one by a man to a man, and another by a woman to a woman. The links to these are here: http://ohmyyy.gt/marrybus and http://ohmyyy.gt/homedepot

The children were, like most adults watching the videos, at first surprised by the fact that these were same-sex couples. But nearly all of them said that the proposals were touching, and that it doesn't matter that these are LGBTs. The video of their reactions can be found here, and it is worth a view: http://ohmyyy.gt/kidsreact

These children represent the future, a bit of which we are glimpsing today. It gives me great hope for our country, and it reminds me that every day we continue to fulfill the dream so eloquently articulated and launched by Reverend Martin Luther King, Jr., that we will one day judge people not by the color of their skin — or the kind of love they have — but by the content of their character.

I am nearly 75 years old. I have lived through four wars, spent my childhood in two U.S internment camps, and watched a nation go from segregation and Jim Crow to electing an African American president.

The promise of true equality in America remains unfulfilled, but with each moment like today, I know that we can be a nation that lives up to its ideals. And I can't wait for all those wedding invitations

-George Takei

Dippity Duped

You may have noticed, I am something of a prankster. Unsurprisingly, then, one of my favorite holidays is April Fools' Day — a day on which I have successfully, and definitively, shown that many people simply do not pay attention to their calendars. Just how do so many forget about this marvelous day when, year after year, we pranksters clobber them on it? I've sometimes wondered if the fact that the holiday falls on the *first* of April, when many haven't yet realized that March is over, contributes to the general amnesia of humankind. We'd all be prepared if it fell in the middle of the month.

Now, of course, the business of April Fools' is the duping of others. Many others, if possible. This tradition has notable variations, including the practice of the Italians, French and French Canadians of the *poisson d'avril* — literally the "April's Fish." In those cultures, it appears the point of April 1st is to stick a paper fish to someone else's back unnoticed, rather like our "Kick Me" signs which are always hilarious.

Now, paper fish may not seem very funny in the abstract. But my Italian-born producer of *Allegiance*, with the highly mellifluous and curiously soothing name of Giovanni Lorenzo Thione, insists that the day is a hoot: "You can imagine people walking around with fish taped to their backs, and everyone else seeing them. But they don't know. That is so funny! And when you see two or three people with fish, it is even funnier." (Imagine that in his accent. It's quite convincing.)

I suppose it *would* have been quite funny had one of Il Duce's generals tagged him with a paper fish on *pesce d'aprile*, perhaps right before some fiery speech about conquering poor Ethiopia. It's hard to be taken seriously with a paper fish on your back.

Victor Hugo — or Disney, depending on your taste — immortalized in *The Hunchback of Notre Dame* a subversive medieval French custom of crowning the least likely individual the village "lord" for the day, giving names such as Archbishop of Dolts, Abbot of

144

Unreason, Boy Bishop, or Pope of Fools. The parody might tip dangerously towards the profane, mocking the church *and* the nobility for added fun.

Flemish children celebrate April 1st in a *Lord of the Flies* fashion, by locking their teachers and parents out of schools and homes, and in theory only letting them "back in" if they promise to bring back treats. This seems to work every year without fail. So I've got an email into the White House to try this with Congress. Lock them out, and don't let them back in until they've hammered out a compromise on the budget. And if certain members try to sneak back in, you can tack a paper fish to their backs. Or just kick them.

In the Takei household, April Fools' Day is celebrated by spreading rumors. The Internet is a deadly weapon in this war, for in a single swoop, thousands or even millions can be fooled, all by one status update. In my last book, I briefly recounted how I broke the hearts of many Star Trek fans with an April 1st announcement of *Excelsior*, a new movie that was to star yours truly as captain of that notable Federation vessel. (If you haven't seen *Star Trek VI: The Undiscovered Country*, you probably don't know what I'm talking about, and have missed one of my best cameos. And shame on you for that.)

That false *Excelsior* rumor worked because it was plausibly true. After all, at age 76, I'm still in

145

my acting prime, and there certainly was a story to be excavated regarding my captaincy of a new starship with such an epic name. Perhaps it worked because it touched a nerve in many fans, who longed for the "ol' gang to make one more film." Indeed, it took nearly a year for some fans to figure out that *Excelsior* was a ruse, despite the fact that I'd outrageously "cast" Gilbert Gottfried as a Ferengi First Officer and Lisa Lampanelli as a Bajoran security officer. Can you imagine how that would go over? Still, to this day, in fact, I get asked "what happened" with *Excelsior*.

This past April Fools' Day, I decided to "punk" another part of my fan base — the Star Wars geeks. You see, I *do* have some cred in that franchise as well, and for a long time was the sole actor to have worked in both franchises. Many fans are surprised to learn that I voiced the part of General Lok Durd in the animated series, *Star Wars: The Clone Wars*. In early 2012, I believe Simon Pegg, who played Montgomery "Scotty" Scott in the *Star Trek* movie in 2009, also "crossed over" to do some voiceover work on that same series.

Add to this the fact that I *did* share a video calling for *Star Trek* and *Star Wars* fans to cease their interstellar squabbling and unite in a "Star Alliance" against the common enemy to all of science fiction, *Twilight*. In fact, this recently became a meme that fans shared on my wall:

It seems my "Star Alliance" credentials were solid enough that I was able to pull off yet an encore April Fools' Day gag targeting *Star Wars* fans, declaring the following on April 1, 2013:

> FRIENDS, I AM THRILLED TO ANNOUNCE THAT I'LL BE STARRING IN THE STAR WARS REBOOT DIRECTED BY J.J. ABRAMS. I'LL BE PLAYING MASTER CETI MARU, A MEMBER OF THE JEDI HIGH COUNCIL. THE NEW FILM, ENTITLED "STAR WARS: GALACTIC EMPIRE," IS GREENLIT AND WILL BEGIN FILMING SOMETIME EARLY NEXT YEAR. IT IS TRULY A MOMENT FOR THE STAR ALLIANCE. THANKS TO ALL MY FANS FOR THEIR DECADES OF SUPPORT.

I had my staffers put together a photoshopped image to drive the joke home:

If that looks familiar, that very image is the inspiration for the cover of this book.

"Ceti" of course was a play on SETI — the Search for Extra-Terrestrial Intelligence. And "Maru" was an homage to the infamous Kobayashi Maru — the unwinnable training simulation at Star Fleet Academy, which a young Kirk beats by cheating — reprogramming the simulation in advance so it is beatable. Star Trek fans who were paying attention saw through my joke quickly. But the name was "Star Wars-y" enough to fool many, many others.

In fairness, I did put that announcement out right as the clock struck midnight on the East Coast in the U.S., so for those unfortunates on the West Coast, it technically was still March 31st. As thousands of fans took the bait, my wall was flooded with congratulations and excited messages. "So cool." "Amaaaaaazing." "Only you could cross franchises, George."

Naturally, there were many who were not fooled, and wanted to spoil the fun, but my trusty staffers stood at their battle stations, ready to torpedo their comments as soon as they appeared, so that the ruse would not be revealed by spoilers and trolls and over-eager overachievers. This left anyone who bothered wading through the now one-sided comment stream with the distinct impression that this was quite real.

It didn't take long, however, for the Internet to confirm that no such film would be happening. And in case some still didn't understand, I posted a simple "Gotcha" as a Facebook status later that day. Fan sites and message boards filled up with dismayed threads: "This is the meanest April Fools joke ever." "Some of my friends on FB have already bit it." "April Fools' Day = worst day on the Internet."

Fortunately, the media and my fans quickly forgave me. After all, I wasn't the only Hollywooder out fooling that day. Director Bryan Singer nearly caused fans to riot when he released this amazing tweet:

> I can finally announce @ladygaga is joining #XMen #DaysofFuturePast as Dazzler. One of my all-time favorite characters. Can't wait!
>
> 5:23 PM - 1 Apr 2013

As an aside, Star Trek apparently birthed Gaga long ago, according to Trek fans at fiveyearmission. net:

On April Fools' Day, it is *caveat emptor* — buyer beware. If you "buy" what people like me are selling on this day, you have only yourself to blame — which I understand is the same criteria utilized by anyone wiring money in response to an email from a Nigerian prince.

The best April Fools' pranks involve weeks of set-up. No paltry day-of inspirations here. My friends on *Allegiance* are masters at this. The composer has been known to plant the seeds of a rumor as early as February, talking for example about how he's been thinking about how much he misses China. And by the time April Fools' Day actually rolled around, why would anyone doubt his announcement that he decided to return there for good, when they'd been hearing rumors of this for weeks. In fact, if you can lead others to come to a conclusion on their own, by carefully plotted hints, you're golden; no one wants to admit how deeply and long they'd been duped.

So my April Fools' Day successes lately got me to thinking: Why exactly do we all so love a good prank? What is it about the set-up and the payoff that feels so satisfying?

For starters, once you're "in" on the prank, there is the simple thrill of having information that others do not. This stirs in us the same delight we might have in, say, watching a poker match on television, with the benefit of seeing what cards everyone has, gasping as the ballsy better with the losing hand pushes his chips all-in, seeking to bluff his way into victory. We are in awe at the sheer audacity of the move, asking ourselves whether we would have the courage to pull that off, or how we would react if we were on the other side.

This explains the popularity of shows like "Candid Camera" or "What Would You Do," where everyone but the target of the set-up is in the know. It taps into the same delight experienced when planning — and executing — a surprise party. This was famously captured in the SNL character Surprise Sue, created by the incomparable Kristin Wiig. Surprise Sue is all about the birthday surprise parties — the secrecy, the cake, the gathering of friends, and the final "surprise!" where the shocked face on the birthday boy or girl makes it all worth it. We laugh because Surprise Sue takes this joy to the extreme, to the point where she has to knock herself out with a vase to keep from letting the cat out of the bag, but it rings true: If planning the surprise is the cake, then watching reality dawn upon the birthday guest is the icing on it.

Another aspect is best described by the German term *schadenfreude,* which means "happiness at the misery of others" (as popularized by the musical

Avenue Q). (And really, who else but the Germans would openly acknowledge this emotion by giving it a name?) This is definitely a universal theme; indeed, some of the best pranks I shared with my fans online came from outside the US and Europe. In one memorable clip, a terrifyingly real-looking velociraptor (really just a cleverly costumed prankster) rampages through an office building in Tokyo, Japan. Fellow office workers, enlisted as part of the ruse, run screaming from the creature, heightening the sense of "reality" for the victim, whom the dinosaur had chosen as his intended dinner. The lengths to which the producers (and the victim's co-workers) went to build the prank meant their target couldn't simply deduce it was a prank. Who pulls off something that elaborate for fun, after all? You can view the video here: http:// ohmyyy.gt/raptor

Another famous clip appeared in a Brazilian candid-camera type show. In it, the producer exploits our commonly shared fear of being stuck in an elevator with the power out. To this, however, they add the spooky: A ghost-like little girl enters from a hidden panel when the lights flicker out, then *screams* banshee-like at the trapped victims once the lights came back on. Come to think of it, I doubt such a prank could ever be pulled off in the United States without someone ending up sued for psychological pain and suffering. In fact, the risk of a full-on coronary isn't negligible. Once again, knowing the lengths to which the show's staff went, and wondering how we ourselves would have reacted, made the pay-off in the terrified reactions of the victims all the sweeter. You can view that clip here: http://ohmyyy.gt/ghost

Short of epic pranks on April Fools' Day and elaborate set-ups, there are also the simply joys of your basic office prank. One of the most popular memes I've shared demonstrated how to prank like a boss at work:

After I posted this, fans submitted many of their favorites, many of which involved filling the scourge of the modern era — the cubicle — with all manner

of materials.

These include Cheetos:

And popcorn:

And shredded paper:

Or post-its:

Or Dixie cups:

The cups are particularly epic because we know how much care, time and attention went into pulling off this cubicle battle. But if extra points are to be awarded, it should go to this:

Others submitted examples of how to win at the "office wars." Here was my personal favorite, which I call the "Febreze bomb."

Before you launch one of these, be sure your supervisors and co-workers are in on it, because there tends to be significant collateral damage.

Finally, there is the this simple variation of the *poisson d'avril* that shows how we all love to see another made the fool:

Bottoms up!

Meme Me Up

There is perhaps no higher honor in the Internet universe than being transformed into a meme. It means that, somehow, you have come to stand for more than yourself, and your visage has now entered into the cultural lexicon as a new emblem of, well, something.

When talking of the process of meme-ification, two images spring to mind, you might say "immemediately": Willie Wonka and, for lack of a better moniker, the Dos Equis man. Someone some time ago decided that these two were deserving to be meme-ified, wrapped up in text, if you will, for all time. This spawned an incredible number of opportunities for others to make a point about, well, something.

It isn't hard to see why Wonka makes for the perfect meme. Cool and implacable, and willing to speak the truth because he worries not a whit about what others think, his every word carries weight. An eccentric, single man (and yes, the rich are never crazy, they're *eccentric*), who builds a magical chocolate factory and works primarily with Oompa Loompas with skin more unnaturally orange than Speaker John Boehner's — this is someone who has probably figured out most of life. Or at least the edible parts.

Gene Wilder played Wonka with such a lilting

yet mocking tone that one actually began to wonder whether the famed chocolatier was ever serious about anything he said. This reminds me of something a fan once posted to my wall: Why doesn't "sarcasm" come with its own font? If it did, perhaps Wonka would have used it on the wrapping of all his candies. I imagine sarcasm to be a backward slanting font, each word leaning away from rather than into the next. These days it is getting harder and harder to tell reality from distortion, truth from satire, especially on the Internet. How many times have I read a "news" article from Christwire.org or *The Daily Currant*, and in my indignance even come *this* close to sharing it, only to realize that it was entirely satirical? I really should know better. After all, Christwire.org even published a picture of me and a bare-chested Steven Tyler of Aerosmith, whom they identified merely as a "buxom co-ed" — as proof that my homosexuality was a sham:

Now from the ever-mocking to the ever-too-serious. My second example of the quintessential meme-ified character is the Dos Equis man, also known as The Most Interesting Man in the World. This fellow, like Wonka, is a larger-than-life fictional character who is said to have done it all, from bench pressing two nubile Asian women at once, to freeing an angry bear from a bear trap.

The Dos Equis man was played by actor Jonathan Goldsmith, an actor who probably never could have predicted that what began as an advertising campaign (and a highly effective one at that) would morph into something that anchored so solidly in popular culture. The gist and structure of the meme follows the language of the ad: "I don't always drink beer, but when I do, it's Dos Equis." This lends itself well to hilarious reproduction, much like Wonka's "Oh, so you..." zingers.

Among the Dos Equis man memes, I like the "FML" ones best because they carry precisely the opposite intention of the original my-life-is-perfect ad:

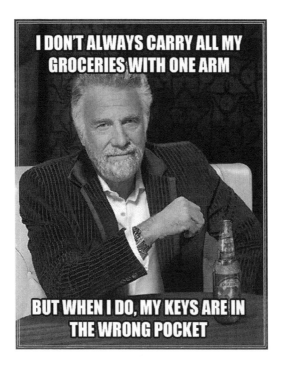

There's something quite funny about The Most Interesting Man in the world having the kind of mundane problems mere mortals encounter. The meme works because "we've all been there" — even this guy, whom people feel they must thank after he punches them in the face.

Here's another favorite:

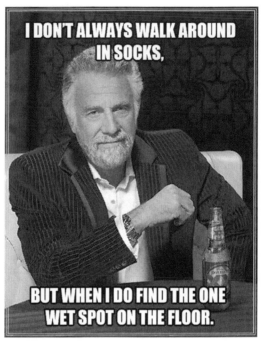

I DON'T ALWAYS WALK AROUND IN SOCKS,

BUT WHEN I DO FIND THE ONE WET SPOT ON THE FLOOR.

It so happens that in his younger days, Jonathan Goldsmith played an extra on a certain late 1960s television series with which I'm so often associated. Yes, he was on *Star Trek*, but not just in any role. I suppose this feeds further into the myth that he is the Most Interesting Man, but interestingly, his was a dreaded "red shirt" role, which fans pieced together over time as signaling a likely demise. The red shirt death phenomenon was so predictive that it spawned its own meme:

Someone somewhere had an "a-ha" moment when they realized that Goldsmith was among these doomed red-shirted extras. Thus this epic cross-over meme was born:

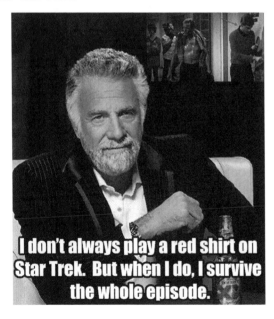

Even Scotty got in on the act, being another famous red-shirted survivor:

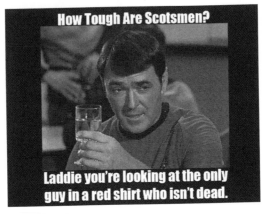

I've been fortunate enough of late to have "memed-up" by fans. My personal favorite of course employs an image from Star Trek, this one from the final movie with the original cast, *Star Trek VI: The Undiscovered Country*, where Starfleet finally decided to promote me to Captain of my own vessel, the U.S.S. Excelsior. In it, I am comfortably sipping a cup of tea whilst seated in the Captain's Chair. Perhaps there is something about the serenity of that moment, or the look of quiet confidence I managed to pull off right then, which captured the imagination of the meme-makers. The first example I came across began, of course, with an actual internal *Star Trek* reference:

It didn't take long for other creative types to get on board. The next version that crossed my feed poked fun at my penchant for proper grammar on my Facebook page:

167

Now, I'm no more qualified to enforce the rules of grammar than the next fellow. And yet, it's somehow *funnier* if someone with perceived influence and stature — say, a starship captain — takes the time to correct your grammar, while in the next moment addresses matters as pressing as, say, the end of the world. In fact, around the time of the predicted end, on December 21, 2012, gloom-and-doomsayers were lampooned generally across Facebook and Twitter, and a meme of me was deployed to great Wonka-like effect:

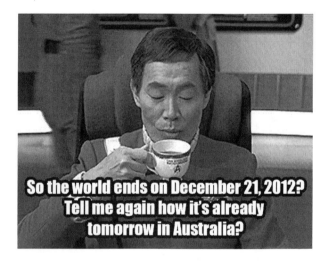

So much for apocalypse now. During the latter days of 2012, I actually had a great deal of fun poking fun at the End-Is-Near crowd. Here's was a coy play, for example, on the final weather forecast:

The Mayan Calendar, and the apocalypse in general, soon became favorite subjects with which to pair me, and not just because I devoted a whole chapter to it in *Oh Myyy — There Goes The Internet*. I think zombie enthusiasts and Nostradamus groupies alike connect me with old-school science fiction, which often dealt with the downfall of humankind, whether by Martian invasion or nuclear holocaust. Here is one of my absolute favorite apocalypse memes, and not just because it used my book cover to make a point:

Of course, I am not the only Star Trek personality to have been memed up. Sir Patrick Stewart, who played Captain Jean-Luc Picard of the Enterprise in *Star Trek: The Next Generation*, has had a few of his very own. I prefer the one where he is gesturing with exasperation at the large screen on the bridge. Fans decided, quite rightly, that he was having a "WTF" moment. This meme was used quite effectively in a recent protest against Chik-Fil-A's outrageous and very public statements condemning homosexuality:

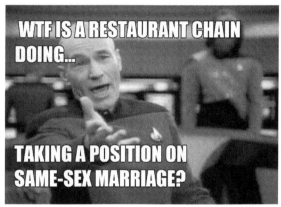

A second meme catches him in a rare "Oh Myyy" moment, while presumably simply reviewing log entries. Mr. Stewart is as straight as they come, but he isn't above playing gay, and doing it masterfully, as his epic and devastating portrayal of the effete "Sterling" in the movie *Jeffrey* proved. Cattier fans nonetheless seized the opportunity and served it back to him quite well:

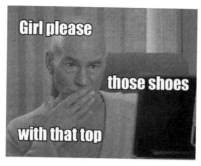

Stewart also recently began to post pictures on Twitter of himself in his daily life. These rare glimpses into his private life resonated strongly with fans, and they at once began to have much fun with him. For example, here he is on a ski lift:

Now, when you see Sir Patrick Stewart set against such a winter landscape, it's nearly impossible not to

171

say it, isn't it?

As with the Dos Equis man, there's actually something quite hilarious about a celebrated captain of the Enterprise doing quite mundane things right here on Planet Earth — things with which all of us have struggled, but we presume our heroes and icons haven't. For example, who hasn't taken out the holiday ornaments and lights, happily humming carols to get into the spirit, only to be stymied and frustrated by a tangle mess of cords. It's as if little gremlins had snuck into the closet and played drunk maypole with the lights sometime during the spring. Sir Patrick is no exception to this torment, but the fans had a bit of fun with his complaining:

Sir Patrick recently paired with Sir Ian McKellan on a Broadway show, "No Man's Land," and they took to hanging out together as pals in and around New York. Sir Patrick put up photos of them on Twitter, appearing in beer halls and even at famous NYC landmarks. Fans glommed onto this unusual and delightful friendship, and the memes soon followed. One even presented me with a particular challenge:

My staffers were quick to respond with a meme of their own.

A final anecdote about Sir Patrick Stewart. Once,

when I was on a trans-Atlantic flight, I was in the front of the cabin and ended up seated next to none other than Patrick himself. I had a moment of double-take, and I leaned over and said, "Aren't you…?" He responded with *his* double take. "Well, aren't *you*!"

It's actually funnier if you do this in our voices, I'm told.

Let's Get SIRI-ous

In the Fall of 2011, the world was introduced to Siri, the new virtual "personal assistant" available on certain Apple devices. Siri gave users the sense that a real person, in this case a woman with a soothing, calm voice, was ready to respond to their search requests and instructions. Although the technology behind the search results received decent marks at Siri's rollout, some critics complained that Siri sounded entirely too subservient and docile in her delivery.

Perhaps this is why her creators took it upon themselves to give her a bit more "sass." The discovery that Siri had a sense of humor, and often a wicked one, spawned a whole new phenomenon, the Siri meme. These were typically screenshots users took of their questions or requests to Siri, with her dead-pan, spot-on responses right below. Customers began to hunt for these gems by attempting all manner of questions. This campaign, which was the equivalent of an Easter Egg hunt, probably did more to further awareness and widespread adoption of the Siri interface than any standard marketing ever could have.

Brad and our staffers on the *Oh Myyy* page (if you haven't "liked" their page on Facebook, I highly recommend it) posted an example of Siri's response to a common tongue twister. This example not only tested Siri's ability to comprehend a difficult sentence involving quite precise articulation, but also her capacity to respond to an essentially nonsensical question:

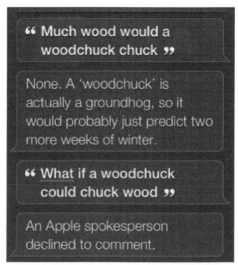

The staffers then asked fans of the page to post

their favorite Siri Q&As, and I sifted through them to collect my favorites. Now, I should caution that new Siri-isms pop up with each update of Apple's iOS, so what once passed for an answer may no longer appear. Add to that the possibility that many of these memes are now fan-generated, and there's no telling what is original and what is not. Ah, the perils of the Internet. Siri truly is thus a microcosm for the Internet and all its wins and fails.

It is clear, however, that Siri's developers predicted that early adopters of the technology were likely to ask particularly geeky questions to test her nerd cred. Some of her responses, particularly to scifi-related inquiries, resonated solidly with that crowd:

"Siri do you know HAL 9000"
tap to edit

HAL made some very poor decisions, I'm afraid. But at least he could sing.

"Open the pod bay door Siri"
tap to edit

Hal... Hal... Hal! Hal!

If you haven't seen *2001: A Space Odyssey*, this is a classic you should rent (or, perhaps I should say, stream) immediately.

Star Trek fans had their fun as well, making the obvious Captain Kirkian request and receiving some fairly amusing responses, which varied apparently based on how the command was phrased:

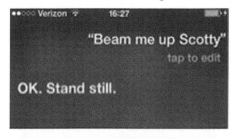

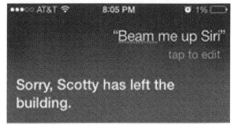

Despite her technical prowess, "beaming" appears to be beyond Siri's pay grade.

Siri has never been content simply to provide the same response to the same question. I found this aspect of her responsiveness particularly brilliant; the idea that different treasures might be buried in the same spot would undoubtedly entice many to pose the identical question, just to see what else they might unearth. Here is what two other fans reported in response to the woodchuck question posed by Brad and the staffers:

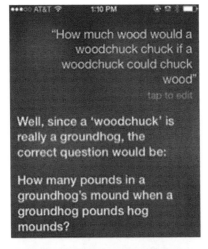

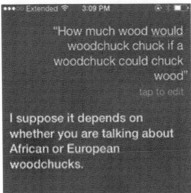

Fans of Monty Python will appreciate the shout-out in that last answer. In fact, Siri's developers seem to have a bit of a Monty Python bias. In a famous moment in *Monty Python and the Holy Grail*, when King Arthur and his knights reach a treacherous bridge, the Bridgekeeper poses three questions, the wrong answer to any one of which hurls the hapless respondent into the deep chasm below. After two of the knights fail and are jettisoned, King Arthur unwittingly defeats the Bridgekeeper, who again asks, "What is the air-speed velocity of an unladen swallow?" But this time, Arthur seeks clarification: "African or European?" to which the Bridgekeeper, surprised, stammers, "I…I don't know," causing *him* to be hurled into the abyss instead. Naturally, Siri has her own response to this classic question at the ready:

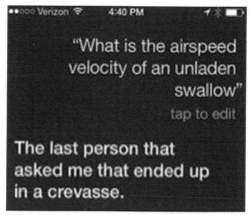

Fans of *Star Trek: The Next Generation* might take note here as well: In a novel titled *Doomsday World*, Geordi La Forge is in a bar where the owner is said to know "everything about anything." After attempting to stump the proprietor with scientific inquiries, Geordi asks the well-known Monty Python question: "What's the airspeed velocity of the unladen swallow?" When the bartender responds, "African or European?" Geordi concedes, "Damn, he's good." It appears some humor is destined to last through the centuries.

Speaking of Monty Python, users love to ask Siri about the "Meaning of Life." Humanity has created incredible technology, which now even talks back to us, but we remain plagued by some of the very questions that humankind encountered when our species first came down from the trees. To these questions, Siri provides responses that are as good as any I've seen:

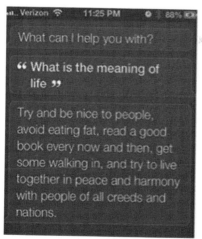

Of course, if you ask Siri again, she might start

getting sassy:

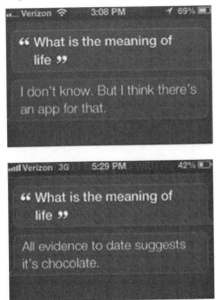

Other deeply philosophical questions are met with equal aplomb. There is perhaps no better known conundrum than the classic "Which came first, the chicken or the egg?" This of course echoes the very debate at the heart of all creation stories, akin to asking how can something have come from nothing. Here is how Siri deals with this inevitable interrogatory. First, she offers an answer laced with scientific mumbo-jumbo (which reminds me of Star Trek scripts where the writers simply wrote [TECH] in place of actual dialogue):

If that doesn't stop the questioner cold, this might:

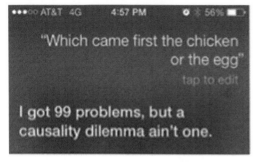

On the topic of existential or philosophical questions, many have never gotten over the fact that their childhood dreams and innocence were shattered upon learning that Santa Claus is not in fact real. Indeed, many can divide their lives quite squarely between the pre- and post-Santa Claus eras. Siri appears well aware of this deep and abiding pain, and is more than happy to help restore our sense of wonder. (Or perhaps Siri's programmers included parents who anticipated their children's unauthorized use of their mobile devices—trust me, a four year old can use an iPhone better than most adults):

Siri is also well-versed in how best to respond to tests of her professionalism, as the following fan submission demonstrates:

Ultimate tests of her loyalty are met with appropriate, comical rebuke:

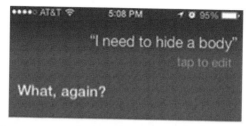

When asked about her own life, her answers again reflect the nerdiness of her creators:

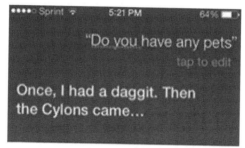

(To those who don't get the reference, the classic scifi series *Battlestar Galactica* involves the near extermination of the human race by machines of their own creation known as Cyclons. A "daggit" is the equivalent of a dog, and one of the main child characters in the show who lost his to the Cyclons had him replaced with a mechanical one. It was the one highly "cute" part of the series that many fans reviled, almost as much as *Star Wars* fans cringe at Jar Jar Binks and the Ewoks as playing toward the 12-and-under set.)

Oddly, when I asked her the same above question, Siri somehow knew to amend her answer.

A PSA for your tribble lovers out there—don't forget to have your tribble spayed or neutered, or you will soon sing like a Beatle, "Yesterday, all my tribbles seemed so far away."

A good and upright assistant, Siri is careful, despite her talents, not to permit users to expect any mothering from her. Those who have sought such solace are doomed to disappointment:

Lately, those who have confused her with Google's newest gadget receive a decidedly frosty reception:

Is it true, by the way, that the early adopters of Google Glass are so smug in their world behind Glass that the digerati have taken to calling them "Glassholes."

Finally, I should credit users for providing their own LOLs with Siri's standard responses when she is unable to provide the precise answer they seek. This produces some memorable screenshots:

Indeed, Siri. Indeed.

Putin on the Ritz

Earlier in this book, I wrote about how organized groups such as the LGBT community are able to respond rapidly to acts of bigotry or intolerance, spreading online news instantaneously and organizing powerful boycotts of certain brands such as Barilla pasta. Later in this book, I discuss how people in the developing world, specifically in the Middle East, leveraged the power of social media so effectively that they actually toppled repressive governments in that region.

Alas, the time has come again to deploy Facebook, Twitter, YouTube other social media platforms to shine a light upon another matter of grave concern: the brutally harsh treatment of LGBTs within Russia today. So indulge me in this chapter as I "go off" on what is happening in Sarah Palin's backyard, for under the watch of its Thug-in-Chief Putin, the situation in Russia is more than a bit alarming to those who remember what happens when the world turns a blind eye toward state-sponsored campaigns of hate and intolerance. The issue came to a head as Russia sought international recognition as host to the Sochi Winter Olympic Games.

First, a bit of a history lesson. In 1936, Nazi Germany hosted the Summer Olympics. Many saw this as a symbolic victory for Hitler's regime, which was seeking international legitimacy and approval, even as very dark clouds were gathering on and within Germany's borders. Indeed, leading up to that summer, the Nazis had been escalating their persecution of Jews, including campaigns to vilify them as the cause of Germany's economic problems, to expel and exclude them from certain trade and professions, and to keep them out of public facilities such as swimming pools. In 1935, they even passed laws to strip Jews of citizenship and forbade intermarriage and sexual relations with those of the "Aryan" race.

With respect to the Olympics themselves, Jews were largely kept from participating by being excluded from German sports associations altogether. There were serious calls by other nations to boycott the Berlin Games, which had been awarded five years earlier largely as a gesture to welcome Germany back into the fold of civilized nations. The U.S. was at the forefront of the condemnation. The then-president of the American Olympic Committee, Avery Brundage, warned publicly that "The very foundation of the modern Olympic revival will be undermined if individual countries are allowed to restrict participation by reason of class, creed, or race."

The U.S. committee initially favored moving the Games from Germany, but Hitler's propagandists convinced Brundage, during a hastily conceived and tightly controlled tour of facilities there, that Jewish athletes were being "treated fairly" and that the U.S. should not boycott in protest. Despite growing concern and opposition to Hitler's overtly racist policies—including strong concerns by black athletes that they would be subject to persecution while there—the U.S. and all the other participating nations attended. Germany put its best face forward, and the world was treated to a spectacle of German hospitality and athleticism. Germany gained a much-coveted international standing, all the while masking a terrifying truth that would unfold to its true horror only a few years later.

I reference this history because there are shades of Nazi Germany in what is happening in Putin's Russia today—but to LGBTs instead of Jews. I say "shades" because the bullies who now run that country have not yet dared go nearly so far as the Nazis in their campaign. But as Stephen Fry has so eloquently noted, all great atrocities and genocides first begin with marginalizing then dehumanizing a specific group of people, whether Jewish, Gypsy or Rwandan. There are chilling parallels here that cannot be brushed aside.

Under Russia's newly passed laws, LGBTs have effectively been silenced, for it is now illegal in Russia to speak in defense of gay rights, to demonstrate or gather as an LGBT community, to distribute any material related to LGBT rights, or to even suggest that gay relationships are equal in nature to heterosexual ones. (Attempts to silence gay advocacy of course are not limited to Russia—we have our own fine mix of it here in the U.S. In 1993 Colorado added Amendment 2 to its state constitution, which prevented any municipality from passing laws to protect the rights of LGBT persons. The U.S. Supreme Court ultimately struck that amendment down as unconstitutional. In 2011 a bill in the Tennessee state legislature would have imposed criminal penalties on any educator who so much as even mentioned homosexuality in class. The proposed "Don't Say Gay" law was the genesis of my "It's OK to Be Takei" campaign, in which I lent my name to the cause. If you can't say gay, I urged, just say Takei! March in a Takei Pride parade, or get Takei-married. Thankfully, the bill died due to public pressure and ridicule and never came up for a vote.)

Unfortunately for Russian LGBTs, their own silence-the-gays laws have gone into vicious effect. Gay parades in Moscow have been banned for the next 100 years, and brutal crackdowns turned bloody, with the police turning a blind eye to violent counter-demonstrators.

A prominent national newscaster was summarily fired after coming out and voicing dissent at anti-gay legislation, and other gay activists have also been dismissed from teaching positions. According to local reports, neighbors have been encouraged to spy on each other to help ferret out "sexual deviants" among them, and attacks upon pro-gay social organizations have been steadily on the rise. Recently, roving bands of neo-Nazi skinheads, emboldened by the increasingly anti-gay climate of the nation, have been luring unsuspecting young gay men online, then kidnapping and torturing, and in some cases even murdering them, with grisly video, intended to intimidate and terrorize, released for all the world to see.

Mutilated bodies of gay men have been found from St. Petersburg to Volgograd.

There is no question that Russia's anti-gay laws violate international law, which holds nations to common standards of respect for sexual minorities.

In fact, the U.N. Commission on Human Rights has condemned Russia and made clear that its restrictions on LGBT civil rights violate recognized international standards. But Russia has only clamped down harder, its politicians feeding cynically upon the fear-mongering of a resurgent Orthodox Church, whose leadership apparently believes it has more to gain from conjuring up a bogeyman than delivering any Christian message of compassion and acceptance.

Against the horrors unleashed within its borders on LGBTs, Russia has trumpeted its Sochi Winter Olympics, with familiar sounding assurances that LGBT athletes will not be persecuted, and that Russia is simply being misunderstood. Defending the anti-gay "propaganda" law, Russian Sports Minister Vitaly Mutko explained that it is intended to protect children from being exposed to "non-traditional sexual relationships," in the same manner they should be protected from messages promoting alcoholism and drug abuse. (Personally, I don't understand how this specious argument "defends" the law in the slightest.) Mutko promised that LGBTs could still participate in the Sochi Games, *provided* they kept their sexuality secret: "An athlete of non-traditional sexual orientation isn't banned from coming to Sochi. But if he goes out into the streets and starts to propagandize, then of course he will be held accountable." One must wonder: What is meant by "propagandize?" Is merely stepping out into the streets hand-in-hand with your lover sending a "message"? You can see how this vaguely-worded "license" is in fact an excuse to justify greater marginalization and exclusion.

I joined a growing chorus of LGBT voices in condemning the anti-gay laws in Russia and calling for the International Olympic Committee to hold that nation accountable. I suggested in *That Blog Is So Takei* that, rather than boycott the Games (which I feared would punish innocent athletes more than it would change the minds of the Russian leadership), we demand they be moved, perhaps to Vancouver where they were held four years earlier and where facilities could most easily be refurbished and restored to accommodate the participants and spectators. I reminded the International Olympic Committee that its own principles of non-discrimination must be respected:

THE INTERNATIONAL OLYMPIC COMMITTEE'S FUNDAMENTAL PRINCIPLES INCLUDE AN UNEQUIVOCAL STATEMENT: "THE PRACTICE OF SPORT IS A HUMAN RIGHT. EVERY INDIVIDUAL MUST HAVE THE POSSIBILITY OF PRACTISING SPORT, WITHOUT DISCRIMINATION OF ANY KIND AND IN THE OLYMPIC SPIRIT, WHICH REQUIRES MUTUAL UNDERSTANDING WITH A SPIRIT OF FRIENDSHIP, SOLIDARITY AND FAIR PLAY." IN SPECIFIC RESPONSE TO THE RUSSIAN LAW, THE IOC, IN A RECENT INTERVIEW, DOUBLED DOWN: "[WE] WOULD LIKE TO REITERATE OUR LONG COMMITMENT TO NOT DISCRIMINATE AGAINST THOSE TAKING PART IN THE OLYMPIC GAMES. THE IOC IS AN OPEN ORGANIZATION AND ATHLETES OF ALL ORIENTATIONS WILL BE WELCOME AT THE GAMES." IT APPEARS RUSSIA ISN'T LISTENING, AND INDEED NOW HAS RAISED THE STAKES BY THREATENING ARRESTS.

Sadly, the IOC has proved itself to be as spineless and hypocritical as it was more than 75 years ago. After meeting with Russian officials who, like the Nazis, were eager to gloss over the evident abuses going on within their borders against a specific minority, the IOC concluded, based solely upon Russian assurances, that the host nation intended to respect the rights of LGBT athletes and spectators. The IOC determined that no action was needed—this, just after a group of Dutch tourists were arrested, held and charged under the new law simply for *speaking* about gay rights to youths in Murmansk.

Lately the IOC has rubbed salt in the wound by reminding participants that it will not tolerate any displays of protest against Russia's laws during the Games. Thus, those who have suggested that the West's response should be rainbow flags, pins or emblems will be sorely disappointed; the IOC is more willing to stifle any controversy or dissent than it is to support its own principles of non-discrimination.

Despite the IOC's shrug of its cowardly shoulders, more principled leadership is beginning to emerge. German President Joachim Gauck was the first world leader to announce that he would not be attending the Winter Games, in response to Russia's human rights record and the harassment of Russian opposition figures. President Obama, who confirmed

he would not be attending, masterfully announced the
the U.S. Olympic delegation would include prominent gay athletes, including Billie Jean King. LGBT
rights groups called upon bars to boycott Russia vod-
ka. Celebrities from Tilda Swinton to Lady Gaga
have voiced public criticism of the anti-gay law, and
everywhere Russian President Vladimir Putin goes in
the world, LGBT rights advocates meet him in protest. In fact, when Putin visited the famously open
and accepting city of Amsterdam, the mayor ordered
rainbow flags to be flown at half-staff, and thousands
poured into the streets to protest his presence:

Putin himself is a curious symbol for conservative, anti-gay forces in Russia to "get behind" (so
to speak). Prior to the passage of all the anti-LGBT
laws, Putin was something of a gay icon for his habit
of posing shirtless whilst engaged in hyper-masculin-
ized activities:

Now, in my experience, the most virulently hateful, homophobic acts tend to stem from the personal sexual insecurities of the perpetrators. How many times have we found politicians or religious leaders, who outwardly profess arch-conservative, anti-gay stances, in the arms of their young male lover or prostitute? Indeed, one study showed that men who identify themselves as homophobic or anti-gay tend to have the strongest sexual response when presented with gay porn. "In many cases these are people who are at war with themselves, and they are turning this internal conflict outward," said the study's co-author, Dr. Richard Ryan, Professor of Psychology at the University of Rochester. The desire to overcompensate and the self-loathing experienced by many who are in denial and deep in the closet are powerful motivators. If Putin and his cronies continue to beat the drum so loudly, they shouldn't be surprised if others start to wonder what they are so anxious to drown out. And they shouldn't be surprised if more images like these start appearing everywhere:

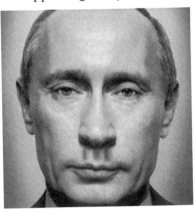

Hoping to draw attention to the plight of LGBTs in Russia, my staffers and I launched a T-shirt depicting the hypocrisy of the Olympic Games being held in a defiantly intolerant Russia:

Through sales of this shirt, we were able to donate thousands of dollars to GLAAD (The Gay and

Lesbian Alliance Against Defamation), which is working with local Russian LGBT organizations to mobilize against the persecution. More importantly, we were able to help keep the pressure on American corporate sponsors of the Games so that the brutal treatment of LGBT persons within Russia remains front and center. In fact, I am heartened to hear that NBC, finding itself caught in a public relations nightmare, has assigned reporter and Russian political commentator David Remnick to report on anti-gay abuses in Russia during the broadcast.

Condemnation by international celebrities, with some social media pressure from people like me, can help bring attention to the issue, but it can only go so far. It is vitally important that our political leaders continue to keep the lens of international condemnation squarely on Russian lawmakers, and to not reward that nation with a hugely successful, "LGBT-free" Olympics. The Olympics are just a few months away, and I intend to keep my own drumbeat going. This isn't 1936, after all.

Meanwhile, I'm going to leave you with the meme that inspired this chapter title. You're welcome.

205

<u>Keep Calm</u>

In 1939, the British government released a "motivational" poster in the months leading up to World War II, in anticipation of deadly, impending bombing from the Germans over major British cities. The poster looked like this:

Some sixty years later, the poster resurfaced and became something of a collectors' item. The slogan, complete with crown, rapidly found its way onto shirts, mugs and decals—ah, capitalism. It didn't take long, however, for parodies of the original to pop up, including this one:

There's something decidedly modern, or perhaps post-modern, about this, perhaps because we now completely expect and accept the freak-out reaction. Humans are frail in our eyes today, and we secretly wonder whether those with poise and stiff upper lips are merely ticking time bombs. The freak-out allows us to feel we're not alone in our inner panic. We just choose to medicate it if it becomes too severe or common.

The next step was for the Internet to spread these

new parody memes everywhere. I suppose I'm guilty for being a part of this, sometimes a large part. I'm an Anglophile, deeply enamored of all things British, like Marmite, 1,000-year old castles and people with double (and sometimes triple) barreled names. For heaven's sake, I'm even named after a British monarch: King George VI. Yes, I'm proud to say, the new royal infant and I share a namesake. (But I had it first.)

Speaking of young Prince George, even his parents, William and Kate, did not escape this meme, as they themselves were frequently the target of these parodies.

As they prepared for their vows:

Prince Harry, too, was not spared:

(though from what I hear, not for long).

As they prepared for their child's birth:

And as the new prince was born:

KEEP
CALM
AND
JUST NAME
HIM
ALREADY

I think they chose a very suitable name, don't you?

An aside: During the hoopla of the birth of Prince George, there was much online debate whether the world should care about the birth of a royal. "We're a democracy, and it's ridiculous that we cling to the monarchy," wrote one fan. "I can't help it, I'm addicted to the royal family!" another remarked, breathless with excitement. Rather than take sides in this important debate, I merely wished to acknowledge that a child was being born in Londontown, that much of the world was watching, and that I wished the mother well:

But back to the poster. It took Americans a bit longer to figure out the "Keep Calm" business, but once we did, we quickly adopted it as our own, as we do many things British. As one of the most food-obsessed nations, this one hit a sweet spot:

This one made the rounds, for we are, after all, a Second Amendment-loving, gun-toting nation:

And we do love our rock-and-roll:

Worldwide, this also became a phenomenon. Special sub-groups of people, such as *Harry Potter* and *Star Wars* fans, adopted the slogan as well, but with their own unique twists:

Of course, I am partial to the Trekkie version:

Indeed, after I posted this one, my wall was flood-ed with every variant of this poster. This included some small business owners who thought they might ride the viral wave of popularity, using my page as a board. "Keep Calm and Order Flowers from Joanna's Flowers!" posted one enthusiastic fan. I'm sure Joanna thought this was a great idea and had doz-ens of T-shirts made for her friends and family. Those shirts are slowly being donated to charities, and re-cycled into thrift stores where non-English speaking immigrants and hipsters in search of irony might pick up four of them for a buck.

Speaking of hipsters, as with any popular meme, the backlash was not long in coming. Once every organization, small business and airport in the Western Hemisphere had a variant of one of these, it became popular to "hate on" the slogan. I call this phenomenon "hipsterization"—when those who fancy themselves on the cutting edge dismiss the very items they had touted as cool until they become adored by the suburban mommy crowd.

Which reminds me of a joke:

How many hipsters does it take to change a light bulb?

You know, it's some obscure number I'm sure you've never heard of...

Okay, one more:

HOW MUCH DOES A HIPSTER WEIGH?

AN INSTAGRAM

216

Once the "hip" folks sounded the death knell, it was pretty much over. Indeed, the below meme summed up everyone's overuse of the phrase nicely:

But one final version of this slogan struck me, and deeply. A friend of a friend forwarded me a photo taken at the Minnesota State Fair, showing a smiling, beaming boy with Down Syndrome:

Having myself been the victim of bullying, ignorance and discrimination as a Japanese-American, my heart went out to this boy. I wrote as a caption, "Being human means learning to see the common humanity in us all."

Little did I know how that picture would resonate. Within a day, it had received over 300,000 likes and 40,000 shares, and after a few more days, it climbed to over 560,000 likes and 63,000 shares, reaching a whopping 11.3 million people online from a single post. That made it one of the most popular images ever on my page. Hipster and soccer moms alike could find a quiet inspiration in that image. It reinforced in me that the folks on my page come for a reason: We share not only a common humor, but a common humanity. To my delight, somewhere along the way, my page had become a place where all are welcome, and where none would be shunned or dismissed on account of any disability. The boy at the state fair symbolized this, and his message to "keep calm" resonated in its own way, taking on its own meaning wholly unconnected to the British government's original plea. We should indeed keep calm in the face of difference, and live our lives in a state of inclusion and wonder at the diversity of humanity.

Incidentally, it's worth noting the "top" comment on the stream, right below the picture of the smiling boy, which I found to be quite telling: "The *one* time I like a 'Keep Calm' shirt."

First World Problems

According to the Internet, First World Problems (let's call them FWPs) are frustrations or complaints experienced by privileged individuals in developed countries — in short, the tiny inconveniences that seem to define modern existence. Mistakenly drinking orange juice after brushing your teeth. Charging your iPhone all night, only to discover the other end was never plugged in. Having to keep track of four remote controls. When stacked up against the poverty, war, disease or the religious/ethnic persecution that much of the world faces daily, FWPs are mind-bogglingly trivial. And yet, they somehow manage to consume much of our energies in the U.S., Western Europe and Japan (and increasingly in other Asian nations — I just read an article about a man in

221

China so distraught by his wife's shoe buying habits that, after she insisted on visiting *one more store*, he hurled himself over a balcony in a mall, falling to his death. That'll learn 'er.).

FWPs first became popularized in the mid-1990s, with the earliest known reference from the alternative Canadian rock band Omissions of the Omen on their debut album *Last of the Ghetto Astronauts*:

> AND SOMEWHERE AROUND THE WORLD / SOMEONE WOULD LOVE TO HAVE MY FIRST WORLD PROBLEMS / KILL THE MOON AND TURN OUT THE SUN / LOCK YOUR DOOR AND LOAD YOUR GUN / FREE AT LAST NOW THE TIME HAS COME TO CHOOSE.

(Parenthetically, I'm always curious as to how these alternative bands come up with their names. I suspect you can take any common First World item and turn it into a decent title of an album or name of a band. "Foiled-Wrapped Bouillon Cubes," for example. That's suitably hip and ironic, no?)

In pop culture, "white whine" began to creep in through television shows aimed toward a younger audience base, with James Van Der Beek, star of the eponymous television show *Dawson's Creek*, and poster child of the 1990s teen drama, at its helm. The shallow angst of the era was so exemplified by a tearful Dawson that Van Der Beek's mug became the go-to FWP meme, with that decade touting its own generation-defining issues-of-no-particular-import:

222

There was a brief moment in the early 2000s when the chaos of the developing world (where the bulk of humanity actually lives) threatened to invade places like suburban America, and groups like the Taliban loomed large in the Western psyche. For a dizzying spell, the rest of the world's problems suddenly became *our* problems. Americans frantically searched South America and Africa for a place called Baghdad and wondered where the "u" went in Al-Qaeda.

That didn't last long. After planes flying into buildings became a distant nightmare and protracted wars were once again someone else's fight, the insularity of our everyday lives became punctuated once more by the most tedious of concerns.

But it really wasn't until the age of the financial meltdown and Occupy Wall Street that First World Problems really took root, and even gained their own Twitter hashtag and Tumblr accounts. Somehow, it became funny for the millenials to poke fun at themselves. Privilege thus became post-modern, as skepticism about the way elites lived their lives increased, along with the popularity of posting about it. In the Obama years, television gave us gems like *Gossip Girl, Keeping up with the Kardashians* and even PBS's *Downton Abbey*, which all held up magnifying glasses to the troubles of the rich and feckless and somehow made them feel important, even as we understood they were not. The Internet responded with classic summations of the terrifying burdens we First Worlders face.

I HAVE MORE CLOTHES THAN CLOTHES HANGERS

Problems in the First World often seem as important to those suffering from them as *actual* world problems. It is, as ever, a question of degree. This is why FWPs are not, as some posit, purely a 21st century invention. No, trivial concerns have tormented the pampered elite for centuries. The Emperor of China legendarily once had 320 dishes served to guests over three days, yet surely some in his court must have lamented the lack of food choices. The British upper crust have for time eternal suffered the ignominy of unpolished silver and mismatched cutlery. But it is America that has taken FWPs to a whole new level. It is only when such great material wealth combines with stunning spiritual poverty, reaching not only the upper classes but across once-aspirational middle and now even lower classes, that the true obnoxiousness of the FWP is evident. The art of the whine has never been more perfected.

Even their triumphs seem trifling:

(This "nailed it" baby has had his fifteen minutes of fame at such a young age, it is easy to imagine that the rest of his life will be spent trying to achieve even a modicum of fame.)

The FWP works as a shorthand device because young people in the G-7 are often painfully self-aware of their privileged state relative to the rest of the world, yet remain completely powerless to do anything about it — and frankly appear to have no interest in trying. The gap between their status and the plight of the desperately poor across the world has widened, but to their minds it's not their fault. Wanting for little by way of material needs, their struggles become spiritual ones, but lacking in spiritual direction, they simply spin in place. Someone they met didn't accept their friend request. There isn't free wi-fi in the coffee house. They've wasted half an hour choosing among too many movies on Netflix.

The phrase "First World Problems" itself is uttered by these privileged folk either to scorn or dismiss someone else's whining — or more curiously, by the whiners themselves to concede that they understand that their petty problems pale in comparison to the real troubles of the world. But does that understanding extend beyond mere acknowledgement? Do those erstwhile kvetchers suddenly feel ashamed and straighten up, shake off their grumbling and resolve to dedicate themselves to righting the world's wrongs? Do they at least stop griping about their insignificant woes?

No, they do not. Why should they? They have now generously shown that they understand where their grievances fall in the line-up of world issues; they're not like those callous, unfeeling protesters of yore, who clearly thought their problems outweighed anyone else's. No, this is the new generation of caring, sensitive, global-minded would-be millionaires. Now that *we* understand that *they* understand how fortunate they are to even *have* such problems, they're free to openly grouse. It is as though by merely uttering the words "First World Problem" they get a get-out-of-jail-free card, and may now continue to do nothing more than bear witness to injustice and

227

inequity simply because they've demonstrated perspective.

Every now and then, something breaks through the haze, but inevitably sinks back into the social quicksand. In early 2012 the world ignited behind a viral idea to rid the planet of one of its worst criminals, the warlord "Kony" in Africa, whose practice of recruiting child soldiers was exposed by the STOP KONY YouTube campaign. I admit, even I was inspired by the very *idea* that an idea, shared often enough, could change the world. How bizarrely that campaign fizzled, after the fellow behind the movement allegedly suffered some kind of mental breakdown (or perhaps he was simply drunk) and wound up arrested for public masturbation and vandalism in the suburban town of Pacific Beach, San Diego. Months later, he naturally appeared on *Oprah*, the confession booth of our times, to seek absolution for his sins. Apparently it doesn't take much to entice us into a quick interest in the rest of the world, but it takes even less for us to turn from it.

Perhaps it is our very ease with social interaction these days that grants us a sense of connection and involvement, when in fact, as with FWPs, there is no real significance to our actions. Watching a KONY video and sharing it with our network is not difficult, but does it "do" anything? Does social sharing around the margins of a problem simply ease our consciences, just as pointing out that something is a First World Problem somehow excuses the complaint? Is it simply an indulgent exercise that allows us then to slip back into the comfort of Snuggies, Playstation 4s and air purifiers?

The rest of the world knows and understands the power of social media, and can use it to devastating effect. The Arab Spring of 2012 blossomed out of the social networks of Twitter and Facebook, and that led to a massive reordering of the region's entire political and social order, including a terrible civil war in Syria — one that now has serious First World implications

229

as Russia re-aligns with its long-standing partner and chemical warfare threatens to engulf our own allies there. Given how many regimes fell in such rapid succession, it's small wonder that Facebook and Twitter continue to be blocked by the Chinese leadership behind the Great Firewall of China.

I had my own admitted First World Problem, a "pet peeve" which irked me sufficiently that I decided to do something about it via social media. I travel frequently and use a "Personal Electronic Device" — a Kindle Fire given to me as a gift from a fellow producer of *Allegiance*. It always seemed silly to me that, long after the plane had taken off, or long before it was set to touch down, we were made to turn off these devices and stow them. I understood the initial conservatism behind this policy, as no one had really ever studied or understood the effect that wireless devices might have on cockpit controls. But after years of use, and studies that showed that these devices emitted such negligible signal as to be of no issue to air safety, the FAA had not eased up on its rules. "I'll need you to turn that off, sir," was their constant refrain. I'd sigh, resigned to picking up the airline magazine I'd read it three times already, or browsing through the Catalog of Ridiculous Items that, no doubt, they'd hoped we'd peruse for lack of anything better to do during those first and last fifteen minutes of flight.

So I did what any deeply burdened American would do: I took to my blog and bitched about it. I understood that this was a FWP and that I'd get called out on it. (#FirstWorldProblems was in fact the top comment to my post.) Like other FWPs, there are indeed much larger problems to worry about than whether travelers can have their PEDs on during the entire duration of the flight. "Why don't you put your Kindle down for 10 minutes, George?" "Is it too much to ask that we, I don't know, meet the person sitting next to us instead of burying ourselves in our devices?" "Surely you can use your celebrity in the service of higher causes, Takei."

But still, it irked me because this was an inefficiency, a useless regulation that was plainly a chestnut from an earlier paranoia long since disproven. It turned passengers into grumps and flight attendants into scolds, all for no reason. So I began an online petition to ask the FAA to review its regulation. Happily, other forces were also already at work, including efforts by Senator Claire McCaskill of Missouri to have the rule revisited.

My timing could not have been better. My petition garnered over 20,000 signatures from other First World Problemers, and we presented it right as the FAA went into deliberations over the new rule. Lo and behold, in the late fall of 2013, my prayers were answered, and the rule was relaxed so that I could now keep my Kindle on throughout the flight. FWP solved! Every time you hear them tell you that you can now keep your device on, I hope you'll think of me and the 20,000 people who bitched along with me. (Some have suggested that in reality, my petition and my blog post did nothing to move the ball forward, that the wheels of justice were already turning and that I and my legion of petitioners had merely been shouting into the wind. I like to think that we *were* heard, and that our government is responsive to us and to common sense. Well, that last part is probably wishful thinking, I admit.)

The truth is, most FWPs don't really have a solution — at least not one readily apparent. What do you do when your boss at work is buying you lunch *so often that your food at home is going bad*? Or when your iPhone receives a Facebook notification *even though you are already on Facebook on your computer*? Or when you put food in the microwave and it's popping and sizzling like it's hot, and then you check *and it's still cold*?

Social media celeb Ryan Higa put out a fascinating PSA on this very question. He suggests that, if you know someone suffering from FWPs, you get them three things: a bridge, a straw, and a full cup with a cap.

<u>Signs of the Times</u>

Back in the days before "talkies," people in moving pictures communicated solely with their facial expressions, except for the occasional explanatory placard. Often, these placards were entirely unnecessary, underscoring what was readily apparent to the audience.

Indeed, some were convinced that words would never be needed to convey the emotions and the stories set in film. As sung by Glenn Close, who played silent movie star Norma Desmond in the musical *Sunset Boulevard*, truly great actresses could break your heart "with one look."

How strangely ironic that, nowadays, with all of the magic of surround sound, auto-tune and Dolby stereo, some of the most powerful messages are still delivered without a single *spoken* word. We have come full circle in a sense, and we have returned to the days of the placard.

One of the most stirring examples of this came from someone who plainly lacked the ability to speak his pain aloud. Eighth grader Jonah Mowry touched a nerve with his video, where he stared into the camera and held up card after card, on which he'd scribbled his story and his pain.

Somehow this young boy had managed to capture the essence of those silently suffering the torments of bullying, and his heartfelt tears and pleas for understanding, backed only by his cramped, handwritten words and a soundtrack, broke through to millions. He'd made the video originally only as a private soul-searching, until a friend encouraged him to post it to Facebook, where miraculously it was shared and reshared until it reached over 10,000,000 people. (Unsurprisingly, it didn't take long for the "haters" on the Internet to suggest that he'd faked the whole affair for attention, but as Jonah and his parents have themselves attested, the video and its anguish were very real. As far as I'm concerned, the trolls on the Internet need to go back beneath their bridges and leave children alone—they are no worse than the bullies that tormented young Jonah in the first instance.) You can watch Jonah's video here: http://xrl. us/JonahMowry

Jonah's signs were not the only viral hits using

signs as a device. People with pets got into the action, hanging signs on their dogs in a series of "Dog Shaming" photos reminescent of how capitalists were humiliated with neck-hung placards during the Cultural Revolution of China. Thankfully the dogs were wholly unaware that they were being shamed. Here is one of my favorites:

Sometimes signs are a preferred method of communication because *saying* the words seems just too hard, especially in front of crowds of people. Public wedding proposals are thus prime candidates for signs, and people have been doing this since time eternal, from flashing "Will You Marry Me, Linda?" on the scoreboard of a ball game to writing "Marry Me Kris" in the sky with a plane. (The Wicked Witch of the West understood the power of written words well with her infamous "Surrender Dorothy" stunt. Few will ever top that one.)

One of my favorite wedding proposals in the past year was by a woman who stood upon a bus while a marching band played below. Not only is it uncommon to see a woman propose, it was delightful and surprising to see it unfold in such a universally touching manner. Here are a few images from that memorable video:

I must say, since marriage equality has swept across the, shall we say, "more progressive" states, gays and lesbians have stepped up their game, and have begun to show heterosexual couples how proposals *should* be done. Well more than half of the truly great public wedding proposal videos that have gone viral this year are by same-sex hopefuls. Unsurprisingly, and as if straight from the hit television show *Glee*, gay people have been adding music and dance to their proposals and enlisting their supportive friends and family, who are probably among the first to realize that this business of marriage will

241

never be quite the same. This isn't surprising, if you think about it. These couples have dreamed for years about the day they could say, "I do," and so have had that much longer to plan it, down to the costumes, lights and back-up singers.

When Buzzfeed.com approached me to do my own "sign" essay on what would happen now that same-sex marriages were recognized by federal law, I couldn't resist the invitation. Here are what I saw as the signs of the times:

243

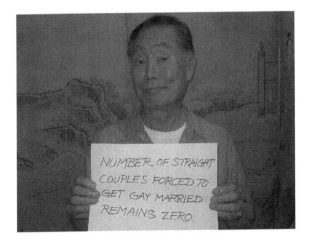

I'm often asked to comment about "gay marriage," but the first thing I do is correct the terminology. "Gay marriage" implies too high of a standard to me, one where, à la *Sex and the City*, Liza Minnelli might emerge from a champagne fountain. I also don't like to call it "same-sex" marriage—it's just marriage. There's as much point in calling my marriage to Brad an "interracial marriage" as it is calling it a "same-sex" one. (Indeed, most people don't even notice that we're a mixed race couple; they're too busy trying to determine which of us would wear the bridal gown. P.S. We both wore white tuxedo jackets.)

245

Incidentally, we held our wedding at the Japanese American National Museum in the Democracy Forum in Los Angeles, California. The irony of that location was not lost on us, particularly since failures in democracy in America had led to my family's and my incarceration for the duration of World War II, and to Proposition 8 which sought to nullify our wedding vows through a vote by the people.

I prefer the term "marriage equality" when talking about this issue. Plainly and simply, that is what is at stake. And decades from now, mark my words, no one will bat an eye at the idea that a woman might marry a woman or a man marry a man. Still, as I mentioned in an earlier chapter, we are at a crossroads for LGBT equality. While most young people today overwhelmingly support marriage equality, many in the LGBT community were disheartened to see so many thousands of teenagers and young adults at an anti-marriage equality demonstration in Washington, D.C. right around the time the equality cases were heard by the U.S. Supreme Court. So it was truly fascinating, indeed, when a young reporter, Matt Stopera (also from Buzzfeed), asked them to simply write down on a card why they were attending the rally. Here were some of their reasons:

"God says honor your mother and father, not your mother and mother or your father and father"

"Fatherhood & motherhood are unique and both necessary. But I do fiercely believe our law must protect gay citizens"

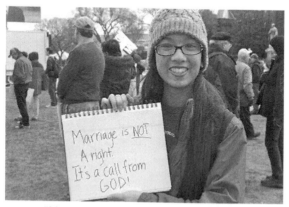

"Marriage is <u>NOT</u> A right. It's a call from GOD!"

248

"I believe in traditional marriage because its (sic) the right way"

The pictures went viral. This was not only because many supported their positions and shared them widely, but also because many saw this as a scathing rebuttal to the notion that the next generation of Americans were uniformly in favor of the notion of same-sex couples getting married. The fight, in their eyes, was far from over, and they are probably right.

When Buzzfeed contacted me to respond, this time, I hesitated. I didn't want to take on these young people's beliefs directly; I understood that they had been raised with a set of religious and moral beliefs that were as firmly rooted as my own belief that another's religion and "morality" should not dictate the rights my spouse Brad and I are entitled to under the law. But some response was clearly needed. Here is my photo essay, which I took during rehearsals in New York for a workshop production of my show *Allegiance* (which explains why it looks like I'm standing in a dance studio):

"I can't be a princess without a king & a queen"

"Many queens I know agree with you"

250

"Cause it's the right thing I can't see myself being with a woman ewww"

"I can't see myself being with one either"

251

"I support marraige (sic) between 1 man and 1 woman because as God
says, I believe. As a true follower I believe of him. And I love him."

"I support the proper spelling of 'marriage'"

252

"Because is (sic) against God (sic) Law is (sic) a deadly sin"

"so is wearing a cotton + leather hoodie. Leviticus, 19:19"

253

"Because we as young people need parents for so many things. And Men & Women make the people they produce I guess I can say it like that and if you put all guys on one island they wont (sic) last cause you need 1 woman and 1 Man."

"Please tell me where this island of men is. Thanks"

"Because God created us that way!"

"Where did you find this vulcan?"

255

"Adam & Eve NOT Adam & Steve"

"I believe it's spelled the French way - 'Yves'"

"Because it's right to do it!"

"Oh Myyy."

257

It was all in good fun, of course, and meant to underscore how ridiculous some of the traditional arguments against marriage equality sound. Humor has always been my tool of choice when confronting intolerance or ignorance, not only because "funny" material is much more likely to be shared (and thus seen), but also because I firmly believe we all, conservative or liberal, need to laugh more, even at ourselves, and even while standing up for our beliefs. I suppose it's fair to say: Those who hold up signs should be ready to stand in the shade.

Tell 'Em George Scent You

In my early days as a social medialite, I often received tweets from other *Star Trek* alumni, either directly or forwarded from fans. It turns out that several other actors from our celebrated franchise had also made names for themselves in social media. These included British actor Simon Pegg, who played "Scotty" in the rebooted *Star Trek* movies (which cleverly deployed an alternate time line device — simply brilliant), and Wil Wheaton who played the precocious, adorable but admittedly occasionally annoying Wesley Crusher from *Star Trek: The Next Generation.*

The annoying bit was no fault of Wil's — the

259

writers knew they had drawn a large target on his back by putting a teenager on the bridge. They even gave voice to fan grumbling by allowing Captain Picard to berate young Crusher from time to time. If you haven't seen the epic fan-created "Make It So" Christmas video, set to the tune of "Make It Snow," you'll see what I mean. You can view that video here: http://ohmyyy.gt/0PhZwT (and if you don't laugh at the 0:44 second mark, you have no sense of humor).

Wil thankfully took his haters in stride, and as the teen actor grew up, he did what many of us Trek actors did: go on the scifi con circuit. Wil did so with not only humor and humility — he became something of a rallying point for geeks everywhere. In a famous answer to a fan question, Wil articulated perfectly what it means to be a geek, and how special it feels to gather geeks together at events like a comicon or Star Trek convention. I credit Wil for helping to make geekdom "cool" again, even giving popular television shows based entirely on such humor significant followings. Indeed, *The Big Bang Theory* embraced geek life whole-heartedly, and even gave Wil a guest spot as Sheldon Cooper's lifelong nemesis, in an obsession worthy of Khan v. Kirk. Fans couldn't resist emulating Cooper's hearty curse with a fist shake: "Wheeeeeeaton!! Wheeeeeeaton!!" (This epic takedown can be seen here: http://ohmyyy.gt/9n2EQa)

It was Wil who tweeted an idea to me which was simply so funny and irresistible that I had to make it into an actual "thing." Most fans know and recognize my signature catchphrase "Oh Myyy," which was of course the title of my first book about the Internet, and is the punchline of this book as well. (If you want to know the genesis of how the phrase "Oh Myyy" became so associated with me, you can read about it in the book that bears that title.) But Wil took it to a whole other level. This was is what he tweeted me to me:

I chuckled mightily, but let the idea slip away. Then some "enterprising" followers of Wil went to work. Not long afterwards, a fan named James Martin tweeted the following to Wil, who again shared it with me.

Mr. Martin somehow had found an image of me

that *looked* like I was promoting something fancy, like a watch or a fragrance, or perhaps an expensive liquor. I appreciated the nod it gave both to my *Star Trek* roots and the fact I was now open about my sexuality. "Set phasers to stunning" is a phrase that many nerds and geeks have since used, and that I have since adopted and deployed.

When my team saw this, they knew they had to make *Eau My* happen. I concurred and channeled Captain Picard instructing them to "make it so." Now, to be sure, we had no idea how to do this. Where do fragrances come from? No one knew. How do you choose a scent? No idea. And how do we even go about finding someone to make, market and distribute such a thing? Stumped. (Ironically, for years my character "Sulu" had been on the box cover of a men's fragrance, but I'd had very little to do with that; it long had been in the able hands of the Trek franchise marketers.)

Happily for me and my team, Wil's tweet became so popular that fragrance manufacturers actually contacted me about it. About nine months later, I had selected a scent among the many options provided (it is described as "having top notes of mandarin zest, Italian bergamot and fresh ozone transitioning to night-blooming jasmine, white freesia petals and grated ginger….sensual woods, crystalized amber, soft skin musk, and vetiver will delight you when dry." Eau my indeed.) And with that, we were ready to launch the fragrance, just in time for the holidays.

To get the new product off on the right footing, I wanted to see if fans could guess what we'd named it. So I had my staffers put out a teaser on Facebook, showing me with a bottle of the stuff, but with name blurred out:

To no surprise, many of my longtime fans knew right away, as they had all seen the tweets and posts from Wil a year earlier. But the rest of the world wasn't in on the joke and when word got out, I must say, we won the Internet for a day. Bloggers and online sites picked up on the product's "puntastic" name and fans shared it widely. Even NPR got in on the fun:

263

DAVID GREENE, HOST:

GOOD MORNING, I'M DAVID GREENE. GEORGE TAKEI, FROM *STAR TREK*, IS ADDING ANOTHER LINE TO HIS RESUME: PERFUME MOGUL. THE SCENT IS BEING SOLD THROUGH AMAZON AND OF COURSE, IT'S CALLED...

GEORGE TAKEI: OH, MY.

GREENE: THAT'S TAKEI'S SIGNATURE CATCHPHRASE, WITH OH SPELLED *E-A-U.* TAKEI'S FANS ON FACEBOOK WERE GUESSING THE NAME OF THE PERFUME BEFORE IT WAS ANNOUNCED, AND THEY HAD SOME PRETTY GOOD IDEAS.

ONE SUGGESTED OLD SPACE. ANOTHER SAID, "IT'S GOT TO BE A FRAGRANCE THAT KLINGONS YOU ALL DAY."

IT'S MORNING EDITION.

Brad, who listens avidly to *Morning Edition*, was tickled pink to hear our novelty product mentioned on national radio.

We had some more fun with the fragrance's name. One example used this photo released by Noah's Ark Animal Sanctuary:

This lion, tiger, and bear have been raised together since they were cubs!

I asked fans to complete the line, which later became the title of this very book, *Lions and Tigers and Bears*. (You can read about these unlikely friends at the Noah's Ark Animal Sanctuary website, www.noahs-ark.org)

That "lions and tigers and bears" puzzle was easy enough, probably too easy, so I tried out something a bit tougher for the sports fans in my next promotion:

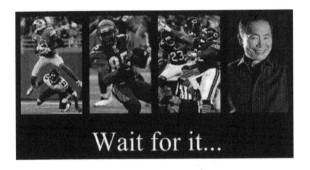

Although most people could piece this one together, I caught some flak for showing the "Bengals" instead of the "Tigers" in this image. Apparently many fans were unclear on the idea that that's what a Bengal *is* and alas the pun sailed over their heads, like an over-thrown Hail Mary.

Unfortunately, I *under*-threw the next Eau My promotion with this simplistic puzzle:

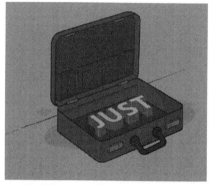

Credit Instagram @nabhan_illustrations

I wrote, "No liking unless you get this. Then fill in the blank: _____ you need something for that special nerd in your life" with a link to the fragrance.

Fans were unhappy. "Too easy, George." "Lame." "Give us something harder, jeez." These comments of course only further frustrated those who didn't get the reference, making them feel stupider by forcing them to scan the comments for the "just in case" solution.

Looking for something more challenging, a staffer suggested posting something for the younger demographic, which he'd lifted from a fan post on our wall. I have to admit, I didn't quite get this myself, even after it was explained to me:

Now, how on earth did the word "pooh-n-tang" come to mean vagina? While "tang" is understandably derivative of the word "thing," I would have assumed the prefix referred to quite another orifice. Oh my, indeed. There probably wouldn't be enough Eau My in the world to cover that, had I been correct.

One of the joys of working with a younger staff is that they keep me hip and current, especially in my vocabulary. They are my own walking, talking urban dictionaries. It is perhaps because of them, and their idea that I make a "happy dance" to "I'm Sexy and I Know It," that I'm asked to go on "current" culture shows, such as Andy Cohen's *Watch What Happens*

267

Live on the Bravo network, and I'm expected to rap using phrases like "She says she's fabulous." Quite honestly speaking, I don't really use such phrases in everyday parlance. Ain't nobody got time fo' dat.

I had the staff put the pooh-n-tang meme up on their new Facebook page "Oh Myyy," which they launched with my husband Brad as a separate page for some of the more, shall we say, bold and racy posts. I learned from fan comments, however, that the word poontang is considered by some to be derogatory by many women (though many other women are fine with it, and deem it just part of urban jargon). I was shocked, however, to see some of the vitriolic comments left by some of the male fans in response to the complaints by women. I keep hoping my page will be a place for tolerance and civility, but it isn't always so, and it doesn't take much to start an argument or name-calling on the Internet. In fact, some fans wrote to me and complained that I did not delete the post or the comments. I found the post funny enough and harmless enough to leave it be, and I tend not to delete fan comments unless they are spam, pornography or hate speech, as I do believe in the marketplace of ideas, and that people shouldn't take the Internet too seriously.

But it is exhausting to receive so many opinionated emails and wall posts. As my own schedule gets busier and the rigors of life in the social media spotlight grow more exhausting, I'll be relying more and more upon Brad and the staff to keep the midnight oil burning on my behalf. Their new "Oh Myyy" page is dedicated specifically to my "3H" mission — humor, humanism and humanitarianism — and so as I post more infrequently, you can expect to see them taking up the cause in a greater and greater capacity down the road.

When I mentioned to fans the new page and why it had been created, however, you'd think half of them thought I was going into retirement that very day. "We'll miss you George!" "I hate to see you go George!" "It's been fun having a favorite gay Uncle."

Well, friends, I'm not done with this new phase of my life, and simply because I'm looking ahead to retiring sometime down the line doesn't mean I'm quite finished yet. It does demonstrate, however, that the Internet very quickly adjusts and sometimes even quite brutally moves on to the next piece of news. As I write this, the tragic and somewhat ironic car accident death of Paul Walker (star of *The Fast and the Furious* movies) was quickly replaced by the more expected passing of former South African President Nelson Mandela, who was so beloved even Paris Hilton tweeted that she loved his "I Have A Dream Speech," and Facebook was overtaken with pictures of Morgan Freeman, who angrily was forced to explain that he was still very much alive.

That's the thing about the Internet. It can raise you up quickly, but then drop you back down into total obscurity as soon as the next big poontang comes along. I've tried diligently this year to use what social media presence I have to do good for the world, on issues of marriage equality and the lessons of the Japanese-American internment, all the while keeping an increasingly feisty and outspoken fan base happy and laughing along with me for the ride. It hasn't always been an easy balance, and at times I've had to keep my emotional responses to a minimum, channeling Spock as best I can so that I don't become as pliantly responsive as Siri or as incurably grumpy as Tardar. I hope that this book has given you a further and deeper glimpse into life on this side of my computer screen (or more lately, my iPhone), and that you stay with me for the remainder of this adventure, wherever it may lead:

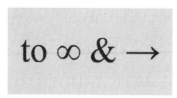

Live long and prosper —

Uncle George